THE CRAFT OF THEATRE

CM1000 2372
05/11
£45
792.092 Sch

THE CRAFT OF THEATRE

Seminars and Discussions in Brechtian Theatre

Ekkehard Schall

Translated by Jack Davis

Methuen Drama

10 9 8 7 6 5 4 3 2 1

First published in Great Britain in 2008 by Methuen Drama

Methuen Drama
A & C Black Publishers Limited
36 Soho Square
London W1D 3QY
www.acblack.com

Original German language work entitled *Meine Schule des Theaters*. Copyright © 2001 by
Suhrkamp Verlag Frankfurt am Main
This edition published by arrangement with Suhrkamp Verlag

Translation copyright © 2008 by Jack Davis

The rights of the author and translator to be identified as the author and translator of this
work have been asserted by them in accordance with the Copyright, Designs and Patents
Act, 1988

A CIP catalogue record for this book is available from the British Library

ISBN 978 1 408 10069 1

Typeset in Dante MT by SX Composing DTP, Rayleigh, Essex
Printed and bound in Great Britain by Lightning Source Ltd

CONTENTS

INTRODUCTION

Bertolt Brecht (1898–1956), one of the twentieth century's greatest writers and theorists of the theatre, founded the Berliner Ensemble with his wife Helene Weigel (1900–71) in the wake of their groundbreaking production of *Mother Courage* at the Deutsches Theater in January of 1949. Newly arrived in his elective homeland of East Germany after years of exile, Brecht did not rest on the laurels of this successful production, but rather put all his strength into staging and producing his own work, and the work of other progressive dramatists. He had already revolutionised European drama in the mid-1930s with his theory of the Epic Theatre, and the Berliner Ensemble's productions would serve as a model and foil for world theatre for years to come. In the first few years of the Ensemble, which were also the last few years of Brecht's life, he and Weigel assembled a tightly knit group of dedicated actors at the Ensemble, among them a young man named Ekkehard Schall, who would become one of the most prominent torchbearers of the Brechtian tradition in the German Democratic Republic for as long as the nation existed.

Schall came from the same generation as other renowned East German artists and intellectuals like Heiner Müller and Christa Wolf. Born on 29 May 1930, his childhood was unremarkable for his time, which is to say it was marked by fascism and war: as a boy he was inducted into the *Jungvolk* (an organisation for boys too young for the Hitler Youth) and participated in the *Kinderlandverschickung*, a programme that took German youths away from their families to paramilitary training camps. When he returned to his home city of Magdeburg after the war, he was drawn to the theatre because of what he described as exhibitionism brought on by the deprivation of the war years. He took lessons with local Magdeburg actors, eventually choosing to drop out of school to pursue his craft full time. He was taken on at the Magdeburg Municipal Theatre in 1946, where he played mostly minor roles, until he was able to make the move to the Stadttheater in Frankfurt an der Oder, where he was engaged from 1948 to 1950.

In 1951, his dream of leaving the provinces came true when he was hired at the Neue Bühne Berlin ('New Stage' in East Berlin). The next year he had his second chance to audition for Brecht's Berliner Ensemble (he describes his first unsuccessful audition in the Vasa Seminar contained in this volume) and was immediately cast next to Helene Weigel as José in *Señora Carrar's Rifles*. Other roles in *Mother Courage*, *Katzgraben* (by Erwin Strittmatter), *The Caucasian Chalk Circle* and *Life of Galileo* followed. Brecht saw Schall's potential early on, but knew that his raw enthusiasm had to be channelled. He set about reshaping the flamboyant style that Schall had cultivated up to that point, teaching him how to make his acting more critical. The two sometimes clashed during rehearsals, but Schall remained amenable to criticism and eventually internalised the lessons that he learned from his mentor, who famously dubbed him 'young Siegfried' because of his blond hair and tenacious disposition. Over the next few years Schall's name became synonymous with Brechtian acting, both in the GDR and abroad. He performed in almost every production that the Ensemble staged. His fellow actors called him (perhaps somewhat jealously) the 'title-role-man' and his detractors referred to him ironically as the inventor of the 'epileptic theatre' due to the almost montage-like sequence of stances that he used to dissect, rather than embody, the figures he played. But he had many defenders as well. In the introduction to a 1965 interview with Schall, André Müller wrote:

There is no actor on the German stage today who is as tough and consistent as Ekkehard Schall. . . . His artistic faculties are like a surgeon's knife; he distances lively gestures by giving them a mechanical feel, yielding them observable and measurable.

Schall employed the acuity described by Müller in what came to be his signature role: the eponymous anti-hero of *The Resistible Rise of Artuo Ui*, Brecht's allegorical play about Hitler's rise to power. Schall played the gangster Ui over 500 times starting in 1959, both in Germany and abroad, garnering almost universal admiration. In one of the most famous scenes of the play, Schall presented an object lesson for Brechtian performance: during private lessons with a local actor, Ui learns the demagogic style, one component at a time, demystifying the seemingly charismatic power that Hitler held over the masses and simultaneously mocking the traditions of bourgeois theatre. Brecht's adaptation of Shakespeare's *Coriolanus* also became an important part of the Ensemble's repertoire with Schall in the lead role. In it he portrayed the arrogant titular patrician who thinks himself indispensable to the masses but who proves to be an enemy of the people in the end. According to Schall, this play and his performance were attempts to work through critically the legacy of Stalin's cult of personality in the GDR.

Like other Ensemble actors, Schall also played several significant film and television roles, including Dieter in the cult film *Berlin-Ecke Schönhauser*, a 1957 story of youthful ennui and rebellion that has been described as the GDR's *Rebel Without a Cause*.

When Schall married Brecht's daughter Barbara in 1961, his connection to the Brecht family became a personal one as well. After Helene Weigel's death in 1971 and the relatively short tenure of Ruth Berghaus as artistic director, he and Barbara Brecht-Schall served as artistic co-directors of the Ensemble, from 1977 to 1991. During these years Schall toured extensively with the Berliner Ensemble and with solo programmes that he called 'Brecht Evenings' (combinations of poems, songs and scenes from plays), performing in the United States, Israel, Australia, the United Kingdom and other European countries.

After the fall of the Berlin Wall in 1989, the Theater am Schiffbauerdamm that had housed the Berliner Ensemble since 1954 passed into new hands. The new owners kept the name 'Berliner Ensemble' over Schall's objections and Schall found himself without a theatrical home. Although no longer an Ensemble member, he continued to perform on other Berlin stages, in roles by Brecht, Heiner Müller, Ödön von Horváth and Christoph Hein. In 1997 he performed a Brecht revue entitled *EINSgegenEINS oder ICHHAbRECHT* (a title punning on the German phrases 'I'm right' and 'I have Brecht') with his daughter Johanna Schall, also an accomplished actress and director.

Schall continued to hone his craft into the last years of his life. One of his last notable performances was a solo staged version of Horváth's novel *A Child of Our Time* in 2002, which Gitta Honegger described as 'one of those rare, spellbinding experiences that remind us what theatre is all about'. He also wrote two books of poetry and a third book of his poems was in preparation when he died on 3 September 2005 at the age of seventy-five.

Although Brecht wrote copiously on his theory of drama in texts such as *The Messingkauf Dialogues* and 'A Short Organum for the Theatre', he left little in the way of practical advice about how actors should put his methods into action in the theatre. *The Craft of Theatre* supplements these theoretical texts with insights from the Ensemble's hardest-working actor. Schall sifted through twenty individual manuscripts from his tours to come up with material for *The Craft of Theatre*, finally selecting four manuscripts for revision and publication. He intended to give the book broad appeal, not just for actors, but also for anyone with an interest in Brecht or Brechtian drama. His book is a collection of practical advice, questions and answers, anecdotes and autobiographical sketches, all of which are meant to support and illustrate the theoretical framework of his acting. In the text, Schall discusses many influences on his acting, including Peter Brook, Samuel Beckett and the Living Theatre, but it is clear that Brecht's influence remained the strongest throughout his life.

'It's funny,' wrote Manfred Wekwerth (former intendant of the Berliner Ensemble), in his tribute to Schall's life in the *Berliner Morgenpost* on 4 September 2005, 'in writing about Schall, I'm writing about Brecht.' The same could be said for Schall's book: in writing about himself, he constantly examines his relationship to his mentor Brecht. It is somehow fitting that his final disagreement with Brecht took place during the last rehearsal for *Life of Galileo* that Brecht attended and concerned a scene that examined the student – teacher relationship. In the scene, Andrea confronts his former teacher Galileo at his country home where the Inquisition has placed him under house arrest. During rehearsals, Schall played Andrea in a consistently cold manner, as a student wounded by his old teacher's seeming lack of backbone. Brecht, however, urged Schall to play a contradictory figure all the way through, to put his figure's various stances towards Galileo on display. In much the same way *The Craft of Theatre* displays Schall's various stances towards Brecht: they are sometimes laudatory, sometimes critical or ambivalent, but always show the productive relationship that emerged between the two and continued to bear fruit throughout Schall's career.

Translator's Note

Many Brechtian terms are notoriously difficult to render into English and therefore require special treatment. I have left the nouns *Verfremdung* (making something appear strange) and *Verfremdungseffekt* (the effect caused by making something appear strange) in the original German, and have translated *verfremden* ('to make strange') as 'to distance', a term that more accurately captures Brecht's intentions than the oft-used 'to alienate', which has an inappropriately negative connotation. *Gestus* has also been left in the original, and *Haltung* is most often rendered as 'stance'. For more information on these terms and others see Peter Brooker's article 'Key Words in Brecht's Theory and Practice of the Theatre' in *The Cambridge Companion to Brecht*. Quotations from the plays of Bertolt Brecht are taken from the Methuen Drama editions; all other quotations are my own translations except where indicated otherwise.

I would like to thank Marc Silberman for his permission to integrate excerpts of this work that he translated and published in the *Brecht Yearbook 28* (2003) into this translation, and for his thoughtful comments and guidance during the preparation of this project. I would also like to thank Tom Kuhn for all his help, Claire Doughty for reading through the introduction and the Rheinische Friedrich-Wilhelms-Universität Bonn, which provided me with a summer stipend for research on this project.

Jack Davis

A BRIEF JUSTIFICATION

Greetings to a past that will be new again in some fruitful future time.

Members of the Berliner Ensemble and I left Berlin to perform at major theatres and festivals abroad; later, Barbara and my pianist accompanied me to solo performances on three continents. On these tours I promoted views on society, literature and dramatic art that appealed to me, with which I felt a kinship. We experienced audiences' amazement and enthusiasm many times over during our tours, and were ourselves amazed by how we were received abroad, which was different from our reception in both parts of Germany. After our performances, spectators posed questions, to themselves and then to us, and when the questions started to pile up, they had to be answered in off-stage conversations. Representatives of the Ensemble were questioned and scrutinised by knowledge-hungry students of schools and institutions ranging from the Sorbonne to the University of Rome, during theatre gatherings, events and congresses in many cities and countries. Because of my solo performances and striking acting, I gradually moved to the centre of attention.

After my evening performances, I often had to answer questions, discuss texts and describe to my audience what had driven me to the point of making theatre in one way and not another. I began to prepare by making a list of frequently recurring questions and answers, taking care that the answers represented lines of thought that I could handle flexibly, thus avoiding standardisation and (above all) dogma. In time, my presentations and discussions began to resemble lectures and seminars. On review of manuscripts and transcripts of recordings from this time, the thought occurred to me to condense and rework the information worth knowing, revise it and make it readable in a manageable way.

Descriptions of my performances like the following justified me in relying on the interest and understanding of the reader.

Peter Brook, *The Empty Space*:

The energy of Arturo Ui could go straight to war.

Glenda Jackson, *Plays & Players*:

I think that all has to do with the amount of energy that we find acceptable and appropriate to the stage. I saw Ekkehard Schall . . . perform a recital of Brecht poems and songs a few years ago in Hammersmith . . . It was one of the most extraordinary examples of the craft of acting that I have ever experienced. Everything that he did was at the border of the possible. His performance had an insistent attraction, wonderful and exhausting, and he didn't even show how much work it was. An English actor would have found it necessary to show his effort. We can accept it if we see the sweat. If you do this, you'll receive thunderous applause. Olivier was a master at this. And in a certain way it's even generous to let the audience participate in this way. But it's a calculated generosity. True generosity consists of showing something and not speculating on the applause you'll receive.

New York City Tribune:

When you see Schall at work during his two-hour performance, it's as if you were watching Brecht himself on stage. Schall's technical skills embody all of Brechtian dramatic theory and practice, just as Brecht's thought and opinions infuse his performances.

VASA SEMINAR
BERGEN 1974

I felt overwhelmed on being asked to join colleagues and spectators for an extensive discussion on the day between a performance of *In the Jungle of Cities* (I played Shlink) and a performance of *Coriolanus* (I played Caius Marcius). The way I prepared myself for roles left me time for little else. On the other hand, it would have seemed arrogant to dismiss such an urgent request, so I agreed.

I am an actor and will talk about Brechtian theatre, or, to put it another way, about how acting can be Brechtian. I will give some examples.

Brecht did not begin as a poet and dramatist who wanted to change society. His political ideas were more general and driven by the wish to disrupt conventional literature and theatre where he found it to be unenlightened and boring. You can read about it in the *The Pocket Devotions* and the *The Devotions for the Home*; you can see it in the reworking of Christopher Marlowe's *Edward II* he undertook with Lion Feuchtwangler and then staged at the Munich *Kammerspiele*:

> We wanted to make a production which would break with the Shakespearean tradition in German theatres . . .

Already in *In the Jungle of Cities* he wanted to spar with Schiller and write a better play than *The Robbers*. At the same time he was trying to write for the theatre, he began to write about the theatre.

9

Theory accompanied his plays and led him to define theatre as epic. Brecht's long march to the theatre of the New Age had begun. Walter Benjamin wrote an essay at the beginning of the 1930s entitled 'What is Epic Theatre?'.

> Epic theatre is gestural . . . The gesture is its raw material and its task is the rational utilization of this material. The gesture has two advantages over the highly deceptive statements and assertions normally made by people and their many-layered and opaque actions. First, the gesture is falsifiable only up to a point; in fact, the more inconspicuous and habitual it is, the more difficult it is to falsify. Second, unlike people's actions and endeavours, it has a definable beginning and a definable end. Indeed, this strict, frame-like, enclosed nature of each moment of a stance, which, after all, is as a whole in a state of living flux, is one of the basic dialectical characteristics of gesture. This leads to the important conclusion: the more frequently we interrupt an action, the more gestures we gain. Hence, the interruption of an action is the principal concern of the epic theatre. [Walter Benjamin, 'What is Epic Theatre?' in *Understanding Brecht*, trans. Anna Bostock]

This is a practical and excellent description of Epic Theatre (excluding the social aspect) and for me it is the best one. Gesture here is not to be understood as *Gestus*, a mode of conduct which is a sum of gestures, but rather literally as an actor's movement, as the gesture of arms and legs, the head and the body, as a verifiable expression. Later Brecht found the Epic Theatre, both the name and its meaning, to be insufficient, too formal. Epic Theatre was a condition for conspicuous, striking theatre, but did not yet aim at social productivity and changeability, which became for Brecht one of the main sources of pleasure in the theatre.

You don't have to be an actor to concern yourself with dialectics, but as an actor I am especially interested in its practical application to acting. The possibility of its application stretches, of course, to the entire dramatic work of art, to everything that happens on stage. Lenin wrote the essay 'On the Question of

Dialectics' while in exile in Bern in 1914–15:

> The splitting of a single whole and the cognition of its contradictory
> parts . . . is the *essence* (one of the 'essentials,' one of the principal, if
> not the principal, characteristics or features) of dialectics.

Lenin names various categories in which the dialectic moves:

> In mathematics: + and –, differential and integral.
> In mechanics: action and reaction.
> In physics: positive and negative electricity.
> In chemistry: the combination and dissociation of atoms.
> In social sciences: class struggle. [Lenin, *Collected Works 38*,
> Progress Publishers]

Taking this point of departure, acting is concerned with the
dialectics of the social sciences: class struggle.

> The condition for knowledge of all processes of the world in their
> '*self-movement*' in their spontaneous development, in their real life,
> is the knowledge of them as the unity of opposites. [Ibid.]

This means that the actor does not play contradictions and
development, but rather contradictions as development. One of
Brecht's directorial comments was: don't play transitions, don't
work up to a stance. If you work up to a stance over three or four
sentences, then these three or four sentences have no clear stance.
The same too for the actor's work on a role: the definition of unity

> (division of the unified into mutually exclusive opposites and their
> respective relationship) [Ibid.]

and the divided figure as a unity appear to me to be a feasible way
to conceive of real social connections and their contradictory
exposition.

It is more difficult to apply dialectics than to understand it. For
many who are trained in dialectical thinking, the retreat to
conventional theatre seems to be normal.

Such must also be the method of exposition (i.e. study) of dialectics in general (for with Marx the dialectics of bourgeois society is only a particular case of dialectics). To begin with what is the simplest, most ordinary, common, etc., with **any** *proposition* like: The leaves of a tree are green, John is a rich man, Fido is a dog, etc. Here already we have dialectics (as Hegel's genius recognized): the individual is the universal. (Cf. Aristotle, Metaphysics: '. . . for of course one can not be of the opinion that a house exists "a house in general" without visible houses.') [Ibid.]

Thus, the actor's experience must construct the figure in a purely subjective way, as if it were more than a figure, as a singular being among other singular beings, as an individual, as a vehicle and expression of contradictions, as a social unity. And in constructing the figure, 'begin with the simplest things', with an arbitrary sentence, better, with several arbitrary sentences that lend themselves to the figure. For Mother Courage a sentence like 'Mother Courage is a human being' would be simple and appropriate. There's nothing objectionable about it, and the performance must examine, case by case, where Mother Courage can be shown as a human being. Other sentences: 'Mother Courage is a woman', 'Mother Courage is the mother of three children', or 'Mother Courage is a merchant'. When you have produced such sentences and applied them to the figure's relationships in particular situations, that is, when you have found precise stances for them, you will discover remarkable breaks and jumps in your depiction that cannot be created by conventional theatre.

Let's look at Ui. Here too these simple sentences led me to the contradictory figure: 'Ui is a petty bourgeois' (for all I care, oppressed as well), or 'Ui is a gangster', or 'Ui is a mastermind', or 'Ui is a politician' (for all I care, a demagogic one). The rule is: no definition excludes another and no definition excludes a moral or ideological bias of the figure (either positive or negative). My main goal was to show Ui in his social definition as a petty bourgeois who must broaden his professional training as a robber in order to survive and succeed in an unpleasant situation. The profession of the robber is transformed into the profession of the political gangster. To make this visible, I show the petty bourgeois in a difficult situation as often as I can. That garners sympathy. In Scene IV, Ui approaches Dogsborough because his situation is hopeless, his gang is falling apart and he himself has lost the courage to hold them together because the police are seriously threatening him. Ui is supposed to be Hitler and Dogsborough Hindenburg.

UI

> Mr Dogsborough. I am well aware that you
> Don't know me, or even worse, you know me but
> Only from hearsay. Mr Dogsborough
> I have been much maligned, my image
> Blackened by envy, my intentions disfigured
> By baseness . . .
> And so I've come to ask you – and believe me
> Asking's not easy for my kind of man –
> To put a word in for me with the precinct
> When necessary.

Ui the petitioner. Having declared a particular stance, the actor should play nothing but this – here, the petty bourgeois, oppressed, distressed – until a decision to change it can be made in this or the next scene. Let's try one of the other 'arbitrary propositions', another definition: Ui is a gangster. In an emergency situation Ui is called upon to play a political role, he is supposed to give a speech. Since he has not learned how to speak as a politician, he speaks the way he is accustomed to. What does a robber or gangster do when he wants to have an effect on people? He terrorises them, he tries to intimidate them. I take Ui's speech before the vegetable merchants and play the stance through consistently. Frequently I will formulate a sentence that helps me get into a stance at the beginning of a difficult scene, I always do so when I am starting to work on a play or figure. The sentence –

never theoretical but rather plain and direct – pushes me into the atmosphere of the scene and makes it easier to find the stance. The sentence for this speech by Ui is: 'Do you want it?'

I think of it especially at the beginning.

Offices of the Cauliflower Trust. ARTURO UI, ERNESTO ROMA, GIUSEPPE GIVOLA, EMANUELE GIRI *and* BODYGUARDS. *A group of small* VEGETABLE DEALERS *is listening to* UI. *Old* DOGSBOROUGH, *who is ill, is sitting on the platform beside* UI. *In the background* CLARK.

UI (*bellowing*)

　　Murder! Extortion! Highway robbery!
　　Machine-guns sputtering on our city streets!
　　People going about their business, law-abiding
　　Citizens on their way to City Hall
　　To make a statement, murdered in broad daylight! . . .
　　Dogsborough, father of our city, that is
　　Not only a name and not only a man
　　'Tis an institution, and he who
　　Attacks him, attacks the entire city.

This is a simple description of Ui and an illustrative one. During further development it will be important to show how he remains a gangster but gives gangsterism a new quality, a political quality, insofar as he uses his profession politically. To this end he takes acting lessons to prepare for a later speech, just as Hitler did with a well-known actor in Munich, a comic by the name of Friedrich Basil.

What Ui learns from the actor must be defined as a new quality of political speech, namely the skill of winning people over, or at least not immediately repelling them. He learns to act as if he is responsive to the people's needs. He places himself with his speech, and only with that, on the side of the people, the vegetable merchants. Sympathy is the order of the day. The second speech (the double speech was not planned by Brecht but was the directors' brilliant idea) begins like the first one with the threatening, frightful words of the first line, but nothing threatens

As Arturo Ui, from 1959 (photo by Maria Steinfeldt)

now, the frightful is deplored, the terror no longer stands on this side of the barricade but on the other. Ui speaks as a victim to other victims, or at least as a considerate narrator or reporter of suffering. The definition 'Ui is a politician' demands a stance that can no longer be assumed and expressed by the sentence: 'Do you want it?' The sentence for the new stance, heightened and repeated, is: 'So it's come to this! So we've come this far!' Similar stage arrangements without Dogsborough and Clark:

Offices of the Cauliflower Trust. ARTURO UI, ERNESTO ROMA, GIUSEPPE GIVOLA, EMANUELE GIRI *and* BODYGUARDS. *A group of small* VEGETABLE DEALERS *is listening to* UI.

UI:

> Murder! Extortion! Highway robbery!
> Murdered in broad daylight! Law-abiding
> Citizens! Machine-guns sputtering on our city streets!
> In short: Chaos is rampant . . .
>
> Suppose I'm sitting
> Peacefully in my vegetable store
> For instance, or driving my cauliflower truck
> And someone comes barging not so peacefully
> Into my store: 'Hands up!' Or with his gun
> Punctures my tyres. Under such conditions
> Peace is unthinkable . . .
>
> Life is like
> That, and because it never will be any different
> These gentlemen and I (there are more outside)
> Have resolved to offer you protection.

This is the description of a different, developed stance with a similar text. The high point of his career as a political speaker is Ui's 'declaration of faith' before his own shrewd buddies. He seems to convince himself so thoroughly and in such an honest manner with his own nonsense that he sweeps the others along with him. It was possible to observe this ability in Hitler as well, who invested himself completely in his speaking to the point of

exhaustion. It was reported that his SS bodyguards waited for him
right behind the door to lead him to his car when he exited from
his speeches, hoarse and groggy. With his declaration of faith, Ui
convinces not a mistrustful citizenry but rebellious and grumbling
followers, the closest he has, his intimate circle, so to speak. Ui the
friend: honest and vulnerable, one step higher as a political
speaker. Speech-making becomes an art; the man learns how to
manipulate people with lies for his own benefit. The sentence for
the stance before the torrent of words is: I don't know what to say.
Or more briefly: Words fail me.

Hotel Mammoth. UI's *suite.* UI *is slumped in a deep chair, staring into
space.*

UI (*jumps up*)
    What I demand of you is trust. You lack
    Faith, and where faith is lacking, all is lost.
    How do you think I got this far? By faith!
    Because of my fanatical, my unflinching
    Faith in the cause. With faith and nothing else
    I flung a challenge at this city and forced
    It to its knees. With faith I made my way
    To Dogsborough. With faith I climbed the steps
    Of City Hall. With nothing in my naked
    Hands but the indomitable faith.
ROMA: And
    A tommy gun.
UI:
    No, other men have them
    But lack firm faith in predestination
    To leadership. And that is why you too
    Need to have faith in me. Have faith! Believe that
    I know what's best for you and that I'm
    Resolved to put it through. That I will find
    The road to victory.

As Arturo Ui, from 1959 (photo by Maria Steinfeldt)

This procedure avoids moral and even political prejudgement, avoids preferential treatment. From his own perspective, Ui/Hitler is not a bad person, he's just doing his best. Making morally or historically established value a condition of acting kills art, and kills love just as effectively. The description of the/a story about a figure must disregard the knowledge of the/a history in an actor's action. Seen dialectically, it would be fruitless and boring to treat Ui as a negative example just because the actor knows about history and the plot of the play. By the way, that would be true for all famous negative figures in dramatic literature, from Richard to [Schiller's] Franz Moor. But even positive figures should not be played a priori as heroes; they too must lose their aura. Not only Shylock must be put into question but [Lessing's] Nathan as well in order to arouse some kind of real interest in them. I play Ui with great personal engagement, I use him to work through phases of my own youth, to comprehend, say, the evil of that time, to see myself at that time as a stranger from today's perspective, in order to understand what could have become of me, how world history – and I along with it – could have developed differently, and how they could have crippled me and at the same time made me into a member of the master race. I play against something, in order to reveal something, whereby I mean Hitler but do not play him. I play the figure Ui – more precisely, the parts out of which the figure is constituted, which make the figure visible and with it my intention. Heiner Müller wrote on 13 January 1974:

For Ekkehard Schall

When the actor Ekkehard Schall stood on stage for the 532nd time
in the role of Arturo Ui
Adolf Hitler, the one he played,
left his bunker-grave secretly,
Out of curiosity for the famous performance
(Whose fame had spread even among the dead)
And sat in the audience at the Berliner Ensemble.
And it happened that he was not recognised

Before his more accurate likeness, but rather became
Smaller and smaller and shrank back into himself
So that from then on,
The other dead no longer called him by his
Temporary name
Adolf Hitler, but only
Arturo Ui.

What the actor intends must be made clear; that is the intention must be clear in its realisation. The actor must be clear about the role, in detail, and must succeed in giving the audience no opportunity to escape this clarity of approach. In this way the audience too is brought to the point of taking a stance, of accepting or rejecting what is presented. When I am on stage in a role speaking about freedom, I must play more than the speech, so that freedom becomes a specific freedom for or from something or someone, a freedom excluding other freedoms, a bounded freedom. When I speak about freedom in a role, I should not expect universal approbation; socialist and national socialist freedoms are mutually exclusive. The audience must be split according to its composition. Having an unbalanced impact on or even splitting the audience is one of the most distinguished effects of dialectical theatre and must be intentional. Acclamation from the enemy should lead you to rethink the performance. I recall how the first staging of *The Mother* in Paris split the audience, one half booing and stomping during 'In Praise of Communism' while the other, the leftists (the Central Committee of the French CP was there), began to cheer. They had to negotiate for some time while we waited on stage. That was a success.

Back to the distribution of roles, the definitions of figures. For Señora Carrar we have: she is the widow of a fighter against Franco, also: she is not a fighter against Franco. She is also the mother of two sons (for all I care with the addition: whom she under no circumstances wants to lose). Sentences for Galileo: he is a scholar (even an unscrupulous one). He helps the church. He is a representative of scientific progress (I'm willing to add even of social progress). Many inconsistencies exist in a role. For Coriolanus: he is a (model) warrior. He is a (qualified) general. He is a (grand) hero. Most importantly: Coriolanus is a patrician, Coriolanus is an enemy of the people, Coriolanus is an enemy of Rome. Everything in its own time, as the preacher says. Each sentence must be coherent in itself and must be shown to be coherent in the play; the sentences may correspond to others but don't necessarily need to. The stances that emerge are active characteristics, productivity in situations. None of these characteristics should be chosen in the sense of a progression or regression, of morality, norms, or bias. Propulsive and restrictive characteristics belong together dialectically; all of them are productive, active characteristics of one figure. A figure is the sum of its stances (productive characteristics). The figure's unity consists of complexes, which relate to one another dialectically, not simply juxtaposed or opposed to one another. It is rewarding and exciting that this dialectical procedure produces unities in the most complex form and vigorously maintains their contradictions for as long as possible. As described, a unity can consist of action and action, of stance and stance, and also of textual meaning and stance towards the text. Everyone understands the meaning of 'yes' as an affirmation. In a certain situation the textual meaning can be reversed to a 'no' by a stance which the person or figure assumes (freely or under pressure). If, during an interrogation by the Gestapo, a prisoner says 'yes' for compelling reasons and at the same time must make it clear to a fellow prisoner that it is a 'no', he will seek ways and stances to do this. An acting exercise: I will now say 'yes' and mean 'no'. In a love scene it is easier to show the reverse clearly: a girl who says 'no' actually means 'yes', her refusal is shame and sham, her wish is to be kissed. Textual meaning and stance towards the text may resemble and contradict one another, but the stance always governs the words, in acting as in life. Additional unities of contradictions can include: stance and costume, action and stage design, and – mixed differently – play and direction (sometimes unintentionally) and, in really bad

Battle scene in Brecht's adaptation of Shakespeare's Coriolanus, 1964
(photo by Maria Steinfeldt)

situations, play and performance. Brecht made some suggestions about a possible staging of Samuel Beckett's *Waiting for Godot*. Werner Hecht explains in his essay 'Brecht "and" Beckett':

> In the Bertolt Brecht archive there is a copy of the Suhrkamp edition from 1953 [of *Waiting for Godot* in German] in which Brecht had written a few initial changes by hand. Looking at these changes, we probably do not understand Brecht's relationship to Beckett any better but rather Brecht himself.
>
> Already on the first page Brecht describes the characters in more detail: Estragon, 'a worker', Vladimir, 'an intellectual', Lucky, 'a donkey or policeman', and Pozzo (who Brecht names 'von' Pozzo), a landowner . . .
>
> *Waiting for Godot* seems to have been a play that interested

Brecht primarily as material. In any case Brecht wanted to turn the characters from their heads back on to their feet and locate the action back on the ground. [Werner Hecht, *Brecht: Vielseitige Betrachtungen*]

I do not believe Beckett needs such a treatment.

Manfred Wekwerth reports that Brecht also considered distancing the waiting by introducing documentary film clips occasionally to show construction in the People's Republic of China.

 We know: *Baal* was written in counterpoint to Johst's *Der Einsame* [*The Lonely One*], *Days of the Commune* in counterpoint to Nordahl Grieg's *Defeat*, to name only a few. For Beckett's *Waiting for Godot* I could only imagine a counterpoint. [Ibid.]

Beckett–Brecht: for me, a classical contradiction.

 Gesture (i.e. activity not action) and text with a conforming stance can also express a contradiction: midway thorough the play Mother Courage curses war because her daughter Kattrin, whom she had sent into the city to buy merchandise, was attacked and wounded. While lamenting like Niobe the plight of her children, she counts and checks the salvaged goods.

KATTRIN *leaves the books where they are and crawls into the cart.*

THE CHAPLAIN   Let's hope she's not disfigured.

MOTHER COURAGE   She'll have a scar. No use waiting for peacetime now.

THE CHAPLAIN   She didn't let them steal the things . . .

MOTHER COURAGE (*she collects the articles brought by* KATTRIN, *and sorts them angrily*) That's war for you. Nice way to get a living! *Sound of cannon fire.*

THE CHAPLAIN   Now they'll be burying the commander-in-chief. This is a historic moment.

MOTHER COURAGE   What I call a historic moment is them bashing my daughter over the eye. She's half wrecked already, won't get no husband now and her so crazy about kids; she's only dumb from war, soldier stuffed something in her mouth when she was little. As for Swiss Cheese, I'll never see him again, and where Eilif is God alone knows. War be damned.

She feels pain and anger, has a real insight, yet does not recognise the connection between her despair and her own culpability. Thus, she enlarges the rift, speaking and acting. To say and enact with certitude something personal or subjective always produces a contradiction with a general or higher authority or order. As an actor you should express this as well. In the preparatory phase, art can take on appropriate scientific [*wissenschaftliche*] aspects that increase its value. We were sure that this was apparent in our performances when they were successful. Manfred Wekwerth, who with Peter Palitzsch directed both *Ui* and *Optimistic Tragedy* (by Vsevolod Vishnevski), wrote to me:

Dear Ekke,

Before I forget: last night your Alexei was of a beauty and intelligence that I barely thought possible. I'm starting to believe that you're on your way to a place no one besides Helli [Helene Weigel] has ever been: towards the great synthesis of acting and science [*Wissenschaft*]. If I were you, I'd try to figure out what it was about yesterday evening that was so special.

Greetings,
Manfred

Many of us, myself included, wanted scientific clarity and forceful vitality to distinguish our acting.

Berlin, 6 January 1964

Dear Ekke!

What can I say to you on the occasion of the 250th performance of *The Resistible Rise of Arturo Ui* that hasn't already been said. Perhaps that to me, my work with you seems to be the first taste of the Theatre of the Scientific Age.

Manfred

The imagination is stimulated and fed by many sources. It must inhabit the reality of the present century and move about freely within it; in must also cavort in the centuries of the past as well as those of the imagined future.

The basic attitude with which you approach an assignment is decisive. In productions of *Woyzeck* that I saw or read about, Woyzeck was miserable, on the lowest rung of the social ladder, a sick man heading towards his own destruction, if not even a condemned man. I was also interested in the impoverished Woyzeck, made ill by the daily ingestion of poisoned Mexican peas, and the maltreated Woyzeck, whom the army did not allow to marry. But I could not conclude that this was to be played as a march to destruction, a path to murder. Destruction and murder are at the end, but before that Woyzeck is both an individual and more than that. If I am supposed to be interested in him and have sympathy with him, then for me he can be only a typical case, not representative of an illness. While it is true that Büchner offered an explicit exposition, it is not the final murder that is most relevant for the story but rather the murder that Woyzeck prevents on a daily basis, not the expected catastrophe but the one that he postpones from day to day. Woyzeck is not a lifelong would-be murderer and defeatist. He reconstructs yesterday, today and tomorrow what has been torn down the day before; he is a model person in a hopeless situation. The strength to live this life can only arise from consent and – be it bitter as bile – it is positive. He can succeed in this life if the one person he needs in order to relax and remain human stands by him. Marie and their child, the boy, constitute this human relationship, and so it would have been until the end if this had only continued. His contentment hung by a thread; for him this small happiness was as thick as a rope. In the productions I saw or read about I missed his consent to the poverty, to this life, which was the only one he knew. For me it was the most important thing, even heroic: insistent consent to himself and his life up to the moment when the woman is taken from him. He postpones his suspicion until he is certain: he catches her in the act, Marie and her lover the drum major, entwined in a dance. Woyzeck's two phases: first, there is the Woyzeck who is miserable but without envy, content to integrate himself into the world as it is. While he shaves the captain he must listen to the latter's reproaches:

CAPTAIN   Woyzeck, you have no virtue, you're not a virtuous person. Flesh and blood? When I'm lying at the window after it has rained, and I watch the white stockings as they go tripping down the street – damn it, Woyzeck, then love comes over me. I've got flesh and blood, too. But Woyzeck, virtue, virtue! How else could I make time go by? I always say to myself: you're a virtuous man (*Sentimentally.*) a good man, a good man.

WOYZECK   Yes, Cap'n, virtue! I haven't figured it out yet. You see, us common people, we don't have virtue, we act like nature tells us – but if I were a gentleman and had a hat and a watch and an overcoat and could talk refined, then I'd be virtuous, too. Virtue must be nice, Cap'n. But I'm just a poor guy. [George Büchner, *Woyzeck* in *Complete Works and Letters*, trans. Walter Hinderer and Henry J. Schmidt]

Second, there is the Woyzeck who rescinds his consent with society and its rules because he loses his grounding along with Marie.

Inn.
The windows are open, a dance. Benches in the front of the house.
APPRENTICE.
WOYZECK *stands at the window.* MARIE *and the* DRUM MAJOR *dance past without seeing.*
WOYZECK   He! She! The devil!
MAIRE (*dancing by*)   On! and on, on and on!
WOYZECK (*chokes*)   On and on – on and on! (*Jumps up violently and and sinks back on the bench.*) On and on, on and on. (Beats his hands together.) Spin around, roll around . . . – Woman! That woman is hot, hot! On and on, on and on. (*Jumps up.*) The bastard! Look how

he's grabbing her, grabbing her body! He – he's got her now, like I used to have her. (*He collapses in a daze.*)

Open field.

WOYZECK   On and on! On and on! Shssh, shssh, that's how the fiddles and the flutes go. On and on! On and on! – Shh, music! What's that talking down there? (*Stretches out on the ground.*) Ha – what, what are you saying? Louder! Louder! Stab, stab the bitch to death? Stab, stab the bitch to death! Should I? Must I? Do I hear it over there too, is the wind saying it too? Do I hear it on and on – stab her to death, to death. [Ibid.]

Consent and senselessness co-exist, they do not commingle, and there is only a single change. The murder is not an act of liberation but rather the end of any possible freedom that he could have achieved or that was owed to him. For Woyzeck, Marie and he constituted a perfect social unity, a happy, enclosed cell they could not leave.

On Outbursts

Outbursts are acting tools and must be mastered technically. They should only be used with deliberation. During an outburst a figure loses composure, control over the emotions. Helene Weigel was of the opinion that even in larger roles more than two outbursts would be too many. She demonstrated this as Mother Courage: two outbursts and a silent scream.

First outburst:

KATTRIN *has put on* YVETTE's *hat and begun strutting around in imitation of her way of walking.*

Suddenly there is a noise of cannon fire and shooting. Drums.

THE ARMOURER   The Catholics! Broken through. Don't know if we'll get out of here . . .

MOTHER COURAGE (*Sees her daughter with the hat*)   What are you doing with that strumpet's hat? Take that lid off, you gone crazy?

And the enemy arriving any minute! (*Pulls the hat off* KATTRIN's *head.*) Want 'em to pick you up and make a prostitute of you? And she's gone and put those boots on, whore of Babylon! Off with those boots! (*Tries to tug them off her.*) Jesus Christ, chaplain, gimme a hand, get these boots off her, I'll be right back. *Runs to cart.*

And the second outburst:

THE CHAPLAIN (*stumbles in*)   There are people still lying in that yard. The peasant's family. Somebody give me a hand. I need linen. *Kattrin becomes very excited and tries to make her mother produce linen.*
THE CHAPLAIN (*calling back*)   I need linen, I tell you.
MOTHER COURAGE (*blocking Kattrin's way into the cart by sitting on the step*)   I'm giving nowt. They'll never pay, and why, nowt to pay with . . .
THE CHAPLAIN   Where's the linen?
Everyone looks at Mother Courage, who doesn't move.
MOTHER COURAGE   I can't give nowt. What with expenses, taxes, loan interest and bribes. (*Making guttural noises, Kattrin raises a plank and threatens her mother with it.*) You gone plain crazy? Put that plank away or I'll paste you one, you cow. I'm giving nowt, don't want to, got to think of meself. (THE CHAPLAIN *lifts her off the steps and sets her on the ground, then starts pulling out shirts and tearing them into strips.*) My officers' shirts! Half a florin apiece! I'm ruined.

Both outbursts were played loudly and wildly.
The silent scream:

YVETTE (*comes running in*)   They won't do it. I told you so. The one-eyed man wanted to leave right away, said there was no point. He says he's just waiting for the drum roll; that means sentence has been pronounced. I offered a hundred and fifty. He didn't even blink. I had to convince him to stay so's I could have another word with you.
MOTHER COURAGE   Tell him I'll pay the two hundred. Hurry! (*Yvette runs off. They sit in silence. The Chaplain has stopped polishing the glasses.*) I reckon I bargained too long.

*In the distance drumming is heard. The Chaplain gets up and goes to the
rear. Mother Courage remains seated. It grows dark. The drumming stops.
It grows light once more. Mother Courage is sitting exactly as before.*

In the production it was not yet dark when the drumming ceased
and a shot was fired. Swiss Cheese, her honest son whom she
could have saved, had been shot. Weigel, seated, writhed up and
screamed without emitting a sound, her mouth wide open. She
had seen that in a photograph, a woman in front of her dead child.

In my big roles I use more outbursts. I like them but I know, of
course, that, like other tools, they should not be used in an
inflationary way. In the case of Ui there is the additional factor that
Ui/Hitler is a figure/person tending to outbursts, in other words
this is a component of his character that should not be used to
define him but must be brought into the characterisation independently. As an especially humbled, distressed and repressed
figure, who wants to reach his goal at any price, Ui needs outbursts
in conflict situations. During rehearsals the figure of Ui accumu-
lated more outbursts than all my other roles. Ui's outbursts also
differ from others technically because they do not use a full but
rather a strained voice that recalls Hitler and hurts the ear. I believe
one should use few outbursts but not be stingy. Don't be lavish,
but feel free to invest carefully, never in a miserly way. What's
more, besides the powerful outbursts there are also those that do
not demand your last reserves. The intense exertion of Ui's
strained voice especially challenged me because my breathing and
vocal technique had to prove its durability. My colleagues gave my
voice no more than ten performances after the premiere; it held
for more than 530. I never scream myself hoarse as Ui. In the case
of Coriolanus all my outbursts led to a fullness of sound, my voice
raised itself to higher ranges, achieved a fanfare-like quality. You
should not use or intend to use such special acting tools at the
beginning of your work on a role. First the story and figure must
be found and constructed as complete situations and stances, as
actions and relationships.

At the Berliner Ensemble there is no acting instruction. Work with actors takes place during rehearsals, that is, attendance is required. During the best rehearsals I experienced, we achieved much more than just a production. The experimental character stretched itself to encompass the idea of a new, rational system of the theatre and the release of social imagination. Sometimes it was achieved simply, though not naively. I was confronted with this apparent simplicity as early as 1949, when I auditioned for Brecht at the Deutsches Theater. I wanted to audition with texts by Schiller and Goethe, but Brecht rejected them, so I used Michel Hellriegel in Gerhart Hauptmann's glass-factory tale *Und Pippa tanzt* [*And Pippa Dances*] and a trifle from Nico Dostal's operetta *Eva im Abendkleid* [*Eva in an Evening Dress*]. Brecht quickly interrupted me and asked whether I knew the round:

> A dog ran into the kitchen
> And stole an egg from the cook
> The cook then took his carving knife
> And cut the dog to pieces
> Then more dogs came
> And buried him in a grave
> And put up a gravestone
> On which was written:
> A dog ran into the kitchen . . .

I was more insulted than startled and Brecht gave me an assignment. He asked me to practise exact stances while speaking this text: a defendant before the court, a defendant before the court of class justice, a rejected lover. He wanted me to speak the round as if I were an eighty-year-old. I must have misunderstood him – I was eighteen! Angry as I was, I acted only with shaking and trembling, as if I had no more teeth in my mouth. Brecht liked that, which only made me angrier. I even had to play the round as a woman. At that time I wasn't hired, not until 1952.

In Brecht's production of Johannes Robert Becher's German tragedy *Winter Battle* I played Johannes Hörder, a German Knight of the Iron Cross who at the end refuses to shoot civilians and is condemned to death. He is offered the chance to shoot himself. Placed in a one-man bunker, he is given a deadline to kill himself – if he doesn't do it by then, a hand grenade will be thrown through the ventilation duct. Sitting in the bunker, the young man speaks a lengthy prose monologue over two pages long. It is supposed to be a kind of Roland's call to summon a distant protector before his demise, as at one time Roland called to the distant Emperor Olifant with an ivory horn. Brecht didn't like what I did: 'Schall, pay attention! Don't think any more about stances and such things. Take a deep breath and speak until you have no more air in your lungs. Then, no matter where you are, stop, take a breath, and continue speaking until you're blue in the face, etc.' That's more or less what the maestro said. I did it and he said: 'Very nice, now speak the whole thing without sound, Schall, only air.' 'And now everything very high pitched, like a woman speaks'. 'Now as fast as you can.' From rehearsal to rehearsal I fell into an even deeper crisis, sank right into it. It lasted until I finally understood that the art of acting is the art of surface, of expression whose freedom fears nothing at all. Even the actor's thinking is only thinking that expresses itself, not the thought. The spoken word is one tool among others.

I learned to treat the actor's tools impartially. The larger the arsenal at your disposal, the greater your ability to transform a scene or an entire role from one day to the next, should a grave or fundamental error that is inadmissible emerge. 'Let's try something completely different': a terrible sentence for anyone who has not realised that only an unaffected relationship to oneself and to the task can achieve something extraordinary, a successful solution beyond the rule. When an insight or new thought suggests or causes a change, and the actor's reason for rejecting it is 'but we had already decided on a different way', then I lose patience. Admittedly, I react to thoughtless suggestions from a director in much the same way. Idiots are hard to tolerate, but those at rehearsals with 'shallow profundities', as Brecht used to say, are unbearable. Each stance the actor assumes, plays and offers is only one of many possible stances. None is to be dogmatised, or overused for sentimental reasons – you should be able to part with each, just like a girlfriend.

It is easy to act a chosen stance as one among many when the figures' effort to explain their intentions and experiences correctly or their enthusiasm to do justice to the norms is written on their faces. The actor falls into the trap of not really taking them seriously and defending them sufficiently. Heiner Müller's *Cement* (based on Gladkov) treats the difficulties of revolution, the disjuncture between its totalising claim and the people's claims that cannot be fulfilled. It takes place during the period of the New Economic Policy in the Soviet Union, after the triumph over the intervention. Sergei Ivagin, from an upper-class family, has joined the revolution. He is prepared to break with his class at any price. Belonging to the revolutionary party is important for him; he feels obliged to participate in the party's actions, which for him are the height of satisfaction.

> POLYA MEKHOVA. SERGEI IVAGIN.
>
> IVAGIN A great day, comrades. Amid the screams of its enemies who wait for it to starve, with a shrug of its shoulders the revolution, itself shaken by hunger, shakes off its lice. The expropriation of the parasitic bourgeoisie has been accomplished, Comrade Regimental Commissar, no exceptions. I myself participated in the expropriation of the bourgeois who begat me . . .
>
> I have raised my hand against father and mother, and it didn't rot off. [Heiner Müller, *Cement*, trans. Helen Fehervary, Sue Ellen Case and Marc Silberman]

It is hard to take this seriously, especially if you do not personally believe in it or if you support but don't share the belief. Yet the actor must do so without irony, even to the point of pain.

Brecht placed great value on lightness in performance, something that was difficult for young actors, especially for me. He demanded a lightness that did not exclude but rather intensified the tempo, power and clarity of stances. He chided me in a note written in 1954:

Dear Schall,
of all the virtues will power is the one that must be concealed most carefully in art. (In any case it retreats behind its gentler sister, interest.) Your performance of Eilif's dance should show the great exertion it costs you. Yet it was distinctive because of the ease and elegance with which Eilif indicated roughly how the dance was that he had once seen.
Your b.

Exertion is an investment, but it takes additional investment to make the exertion invisible. The visible form of successful exertion is lightness, is 'the ease and elegance'. Exertion does not allow the audience to enjoy in a relaxed way, and the audience's pleasure is the criterion of an actor's mastery.

For it is a peculiarity of means employed by the theatre that they communicate insights and impulses in the form of pleasures; and that the depth of the latter corresponds to the depth of the former. [Brecht, Die Straßenszene]

And here insights and impulses refer to those brought forth in the audience. The actor must plan them and the mastery of his craft gives him the means to trigger them. The actor should work on this mastery beyond the respective role for which he is preparing. I call this 'working on the foundations of the profession', on voice, body and useful knowledge. Talent is a prerequisite, everything else – ability, success, mastery – must be earned. For me the tendency and intensity of an actor's development is more important than talent. Lightness should not be confused with personal naturalness. Lightness reinforces the naturalness of the stage figure. Only in this way can a particular stance [Verhalten] become one among many possible other stances. The result is not an agile person but an agile actor; it is the presentation of the essential simplicity of a figure, which includes naturalness and unnaturalness as well as social determination. Passion must be part of lightness as well. In an essay Brecht criticises the 'disciples of conventional drama':

> The plot carries them along, but not in the right direction. The passion is significant, but it is not ignited by the right issue.

It is in this sense that I mean passion should not lack the proper occasion.

Brecht demanded simpler speaking; we thought to ourselves that it was almost plain. On the other hand, he got us to sing, dance, to move acrobatically, ceremonially, or spontaneously in the fashion of each period (or what we imagined it to be). Again and again he demanded lightness. For our London tour in 1956 he hung up a notice:

Letter to the members of the Berliner Ensemble
For the London tour

For the London tour we must keep two things in mind. First, to most of the spectators we are presenting only a pantomime, a kind of silent film on the stage, since they cannot understand German. (In Paris we had a festival audience, an international audience – and we only played for a few days.) Second, there is an old prejudice in England about German art (literature, painting, music) that it is heavy, slow, long-winded, 'pedestrian'.

Therefore we must act with speed, lightness and energy. It is not a matter of rushing but of hurrying, not only acting fast but also thinking fast. We must have the speed of reading rehearsals, but with a quiet energy, adding our own playfulness. Responses should not be offered with any hesitation, as you would offer your own last pair of shoes to someone, but rather they should be tossed back like balls. The audience must notice that we are a collective of artists working together to transmit stories, ideas, pieces of art to the public.

Good work!

3 August 1956

It is also possible to avoid unnecessary aspects of certain topics through lightness. Homosexuality, for example, loses its whiff of aberrance or even unnaturalness when shown but not amplified, performed but not dwelled on. In *In the Jungle of Cities*, 'the fight between two men in the gigantic city of Chicago', the audience recognises and constantly observes it: Shlink says directly to Garga, 'Brace yourself: I love you.' The love between two men does not have to be amplified (unless it must be dramaturgically emphasised, which is not the case here). We perceive it as a given, like the love between a man and a woman, and we accept it. In order to resist a certain audience expectation, we must present the real problems in the play – separating and binding the two protagonists – with particular lightness and humour so that their love is on the one hand not simply criminalised and on the other the intimate human relationship is accepted without frivolity. Brecht writes in 'On Looking Through My First Plays' in the 1950s:

> My memories of writing the play *In the Jungle of Cities* are far from clear, but at least I remember the desires and ideas with which I was seized. In *The Robbers* [Schiller] there is a most furious, destructive and desperate fight over a bourgeois inheritance, using partly non-bourgeois means. What interested me about this fight was its fury, and because it was a time (early 1920s) when I appreciated sport, and boxing in particular, as one of the 'great mythical diversions of the giant cities on the other side of the herring pond', I wanted my new play to show the conclusion of a 'fight for fighting's sake', a fight with no objective except to decide who is the 'the better man' . . .
>
> My play was meant to deal with this pure enjoyment of fighting.

Hans-Peter Reinecke and I wanted to discover this 'enjoyment' by trying to show the pleasure that arises if one inflicts pain on oneself or another through a chosen word, without gesture, only sitting quietly across from one another on the floor. Here the pain that is expected and felt determines the following answer or next reply and once again pleasurably hurts (and should hurt) both the addressee and the addresser. No respect is shown for the truth of

As Shlink in Brecht's In the Jungle of Cities *in 1971 (photo by Maria Steinfeldt)*

these feelings: this truth remains a silent undercurrent in the scene, but assuming it is there, it gives the dialogue the lightness which is needed in order to approach the point of mortal danger.

A deserted tent, formerly used by railroad workers, in the gravel pits of Lake Michigan, 19 November 1915, before 2 a.m.

GARGA   You've always been alone?

SHLINK   Forty years.

GARGA   And now, towards the end, you've succumbed to the black plague of this planet, the lust for human contact.

SHLINK (*smiling*)   Through enmity?

GARGA   Through enmity.

SHLINK   Then you understand that we're comrades, comrades in a metaphysical conflict . . .

Here is the ledger of your lumber business; it begins where the ink was once poured over the figures.

GARGA   You've been carrying it next to your skin? Open it yourself, it's sure to be filthy. (*He reads.*) A clean account. Nothing but withdrawals. On the seventeenth: the lumber deal, $25,000 to Garga. Just above: $10 for clothing. Below: $22 for Mary Garga, 'our' sister. At the very end: the whole business burned to the ground again. – I can't sleep any more. I'll be glad when you're covered with quicklime.

SHLINK   Don't deny the past, George! What's an account? Remember the question we raised. Brace yourself: I love you.

The more lightness that accrues to a production in the course of time (at the premiere it won't yet be easy), the more it will improve overall. The high point of lightness is the actor's dance between tragedy and comedy. It is the sovereign ability to make a comic point in dramatic scenes. Dry, effortless speech is necessary for all of this.

A turning point in life, a one-time decision, and a false one at that, leading to an abyss – this is the stuff of scenes that I like. Such a scene – which calls for the grandiose feeling of finally speaking the truth, of finally venting anger, contempt or hate – can only be played with a sense of unequalled relief. As if they have become idiosyncrasies, all negative experiences claim (do not have) the honour, in the literal sense of the word, to free themselves, to escape into the blue, to ride off into nothingness, to articulate themselves irrevocably. They are assimilated with the lightness of exhaling, of the morning dawn, and of (long forgotten) innocence, with the cheerfulness of a (corrupted) heart, of spring and (feigned) ignorance. Coriolanus does that, when called before the tribunes and citizens. He goes forth as if walking on clouds, towards Antium, betrayal and death. Oh joy of tragedy, lightness!

Rome. The Forum.

SICINIUS. BRUTUS. CITIZENS. AN AEDILE.

Enter CORIOLANUS, MENENIUS, COMINIUS *and senators.*

SICINIUS

    You are accused of trying to overthrow
    The tribunes of the people and to seize
    A tyrant's power. Hence of treason
    Against the people.

CORIOLANUS   Treason!

MENENIUS

    Easy, now!

COMINIUS

    You promised! . . .

CORIOLANUS

    Call me a traitor? Why, you dog
    Of a tribune, you tribune of dogs. You lump
    Of filth! You scoundrel hungry for my death!
    You throat clogged fast with lies! . . .

COMINIUS

    Calm yourself, you know . . .

CORIOLANUS

    Don't tell me what I know. Let them hurl
    Me down from the steep Tarpeian Rock, or send
    Me off to exile, or whatever else they

Can think of. I'll not buy their mercy with
So much as one soft word, not even a
'Good morning.'
SICINIUS
                That condemns you. In the people's
Name, we the tribunes banish you from Rome
And warn you on pain of being hurled
From the Tarpeian Rock, never again
To enter the city gates . . .
CORIOLANUS
You pack of common curs, I hate your breath
More than the reek of putrid swamps, and value
Your love no more than the carcasses of unburied
Enemies. I banish you!
Stay here in Rome, shaking with fear, shitting
In your pants whenever a plume of unfamiliar
Colour appears outside the gates.
The power to banish your defenders till
Your ignorance (which sees no farther than
Its nose) sends everyone away but you
Who have always been your cruellest enemies
And in the end delivers you to some
Nation that takes the city without striking
A blow. Despising Rome on your account
I turn my back on it. There is a world
Elsewhere. [Brecht's adaptation of Coriolanus]

The personality of an actor remains in the spectators'
memories. This presence creates attention for the figure, makes
it humanly relevant. The art of acting is not about creating
human beings but rather it is the sum of deliberations, stances
and gestures in constructed situations. This sum is conveyed to
the audience as a single figure if it is assembled successfully.
Whether the components come together as a whole does not
have to overly concern the actor; his responsibility lies in the

truthfulness of the components. The actor needs a space, the stage, on which he can feel free to act and decide as the highest authority, without endangering the agreements that hold a production together and help the individual become a part of the collective achievement.

Answers to Questions from the Audience

Unity
If parts appear as parts, and not as parts of a whole, then an actor has worked undialectically. When a great violinist plays, he becomes one with his violin, forming a unity with it that expresses itself musically through contradiction. A sophisticated unity consists of many parts and must be lively.

Process
Art as a process sets great diversity free, reality struggles to catch up and previous understanding shatters. The process of art always becomes the process of the individual. Brecht on this topic:

> More and more, the *individual* seems to us a contradictory, continuously developing complex, similar to a mass. It may appear from the outside to be a unity, but is for this reason a more-or-less battle-torn multitude in which different tendencies win the upper hand, rendering every action a compromise. [Brecht, GW 20, 'Notizen über Individuum und Masse']

Empathy
You can certainly use empathy. I use it when I want to lure the audience on to the wrong track; I seduce them with a true passion and abandon them at precisely the moment when they have accepted the sympathy or antipathy of which – viewed objectively – they actually should be ashamed. I discredit thereby my own previous acting and achieve what I intend.

Personality
The actor's personality has nothing directly to do with preparation
for a role, and should not be brought into the role, even if it is
finally expressed there. Personality is present and has been worked
out in life, and this is where it must articulate itself. In Goethe's
Tasso, Leonore Sanvitale says:

> A talent in tranquillity is formed,
> A character in the turbulence of affairs.
> [*Torquato Tasso*, Goethe, *Collected Works 8*, Suhrkamp]

A Figure's Character
You shouldn't start work on a role with an ideal portrait of a figure
or his imagined character. That's putting the cart before the horse.
The later figure's character, or even the entire presentation of the
later figure, is something secondary, really something that does
not concern the actor any more. The figure materialises and
becomes whatever the spectator is able to take from the total
performance, whatever is transferred to him.

Naturalism
To us, naturalistic representation is not suspect in the general
sense of being too mimetic, but rather only because it does not
allow for a critical stance.

Beginning Work on a Role
Extract your own story and write it down. You must force yourself
to fix the story in writing; it is more precise than the narrative. And
do not use a description or formulation from the text. You must
undermine the obvious structure and produce a second story
[*Fabel*], a personal one. What really happens? Do not avoid the
difficulties. Admit your ignorance and make corrections; get used
to the snail's pace of comprehension. Accept nothing as self-
evident (who would need a play for that?). Recognise the
authorities and dismiss them. Greet each inconsistency you find

with the utmost care; do not allow confusion or chaos to be explained away. If something does not fit together, take it to rehearsal and try it out, and privilege nothing – that which exists must explain itself without being prejudged as good or bad. The modest result may also be the right one; failure may be the successful explanation of the given. First, confuse the project; it is the only way to force yourself to find a solution, and it must be a practical one and then dissolve itself into thin air. The solution does not seek clarity. What your figure can offer will be helpless; its success will be joyously accepted and reluctantly shared.

Addendum

Just as you can transpose notes or sequences of notes, you can also transpose thoughts and sequences of thoughts; for example, philosophical thoughts from social reality into imagined aesthetic structures, that is, into the realm of posited figures. Professor Wolfgang Heise gave me this assignment when he presented me with Marx's theses on Feuerbach. If you apply them or transfer them to dramatic art, you come to the realisation: critique has to be contained in the thing itself, that is, for and within acting, just like what Marx says about philosophers in the world.

> I
>
> The chief defect of all previous materialism – that of Feuerbach included — is that things [*Gegenstand*], reality, sensuousness are conceived only in the form of the *object, or of contemplation*, but not as *sensuous human activity, practice*, not subjectively. . . . Hence he [Feuerbach] does not grasp the significance of 'revolutionary', of 'practical-critical', activity. [Karl Marx. *Marx and Engels Collected Works, Volume 5*, International Publishers]

I take from Marx that the actor understands the figure or character metaphorically, as sensuous human activity or practice, i.e. subjectively, and so conceives of it in its practical and critical revolutionary activity. The figure is practised and presented as a certain sum of actions, which presuppose changes both within the figure itself, and outside it. Take note: every action is a reaction.

3

The materialist doctrine concerning the changing of circumstances and upbringing forgets that circumstances are changed by men and that the educator must himself be educated. This doctrine must, therefore, divide society into two parts, one of which is superior to society.

The coincidence of the changing of circumstances and of human activity or self-change can be conceived and rationally understood only as *revolutionary practice*. [Ibid.]

Putting together a sum of all actions, whether in the plot of a play or an historical development that comes into being directly, means creating a universe that is seemingly closed and requires nothing outside itself. A work of art is a closed universe. Brecht writes in *The Messingkauf Dialogues*: 'The only way to clarify your incidents is by other incidents.'

Seen in this way, actors can never stand outside their roles, even if they barely use empathy, because they must continuously engage cleverly and robustly with the activities of their roles. And these actions (or respective reactions) are made subjective in that the actor gives them his own external appearance and expressive possibilities. The philosophical conclusion to be drawn from all of this would be that the idea cannot be separated from the reality being represented, that what is human is continuously being defined.

6

. . . But the essence of man is no abstraction inherent in each single individual. In its reality it is the ensemble of social relations. [Ibid.]

The figure's logic is intrinsic to the logic of the play.

Addendum Two

Concerning recitation: the art of recitation is stricter than the art of acting. Brecht writes in his journal:

> 17 jan 42
> in the evening visit ludwig hardt. he is an old-style reciter, who loads each word with atmosphere, a kind of accompaniment ('stuffed words, with apple sauce'). i say i'm for an open, unparsonical declamation, avoiding all sonorous cadenzas, crescendos and tremolos.

One could think that Brecht agrees with Goethe's 'On Acting', in the part titled 'Recitation and Declamation':

> By recitation we mean a method of delivery that lies halfway between passionless, detached speech and speech that is highly emotional; it does not soar with feeling, yet it is not completely devoid of expression. The audience must always be aware that the actor is simply reciting a text.

To be sure, passages calling for recitation must be presented with the appropriate expression of the sensations and feelings which the poem inspires in the reader through its content. But this must be done with moderation and without the complete surrender to the role that is called for in declamation.

One can be certain, however, that Brecht does not agree with Goethe when Goethe describes a style of recitation similar to one that Hardt may have used. This style of recitation appeals to me, however, provided it is mixed with a measure of intelligence.

> However, declamation, or heightened recitation is quite a different matter. Here you must relinquish your innate character, disown your nature and enter completely into the situation and mood of the person whose part you are speaking. The words that you say must be delivered with energy and the liveliest expression, so that it seems that you are actually experiencing every emotion. [J. W. Goethe, *Collected Works 3*, Suhrkamp]

I like to go all out when I recite poems or sing songs – albeit in a premeditated and technically masterful way. But I have to say that what practically disgusts me is when actors read poems to their audience. Since they are too lazy to take on the effort of memorisation and not artist enough to want to offer their own work of art through free recitation, they are tied to the text and only reach a superficial level of artistry and interpretation, one that is not filtered through their entire personality, not won out of necessity. I read further in the Brecht's journal:

> hardt complains that in a hall this poem would call for some comment. i find comments a good thing, because they separate the poems from one another, equip them with a *V-effekt* and set them on firm ground. poems are unsociable creatures. on the whole they are disagreeable when herded together, and they get on badly with one another. also their colours rub off on each other and they keep chipping into one another's conversation. [Translation altered]

I agree with that. I like to talk between poems, but only briefly. I comment a bit. But an evening of poems can be polemical even without commentary, merely in the way it is put together. In most cases, recitation differs from acting at the theatre in that it is less subjective. The metric form (and irregular rhythm) must be kept more strictly and the poet's message declaimed more directly. The poet's message and the actor's interpretation should not get in the way of one other, which is acceptable when acting (and is usually the case) but shouldn't be intended from the start. A role is interpreted through stances, a poem is interpreted through agreement with the content and word choice. The exceptions are ballads and character-songs or -poems. Both exceptions occur in Brecht's work: 'Children's Crusade' (Brecht was very generous, or even lax with the term 'ballad') and 'The Song of Surabaya Johnny'. Descriptions of nature, mood poems and reflective poems make up the largest part of poetry, which can extend itself into the realm of the epic and encompass both inferno and utopia. To these genres belong instructive poems [*Lehrgedichte*] one of which, Lucretius' 'On the Nature of Things', inspired Brecht to plan and sketch out his own 'On Human Nature (On the Unnaturalness of Bourgeois Relations)'. It remained fragmentary, influencing 'The Manifesto', a versification, in hexameter, of the introduction and first chapter of the *Communist Manifesto* by Marx and Engels, about which Brecht wrote:

> As a pamphlet, 'The Manifesto' is already a work of art. But it seems possible to me now, one hundred years later . . ., to renew its propagandistic effect by altering its pamphlet-like character.

The Manifesto

Wars are destroying the world, & the ruins are visibly haunted
By an enormous spectre, not simply born of war.
In peace it could already be sighted, terror to the rulers
But friend to the children of the slums . . .
It speaks in many
Tongues, in all of them. And in many it holds its tongue.
It sits as a guest of honour in hovels, a headache in villas,
It has come to change all things & stay for ever, its name is
Communism. . . .
The house does not exist for dwelling, the cloth for dressing
Nor the bread for stilling hunger: they must bring Profit. . . .
chaos results from the bourgeoisie's
Plans, the more plans the more chaos . . .
The new class
It raised, the proletariat, will bring it down . . .
The vast majority is in this movement, & when it rules
This is no longer ruling but the suppression of rule. . . .
The proletarians, lowest
Level of society, must, in order to rise, smash
Into pieces the whole social structure with all its upper levels.
The proletariat can only throw off its special class
Servitude by throwing off the servitude of all.
[Darko Suvin, 'The Manifesto' in 'Socialism and Democracy', vol. 16, no. 1]

Here, victory or the promise of victory is felt to be part of the historical process and elevated to a victory for all of humanity. Homer and Mayakovsky, Whitman, Eliot and Neruda lived in their works from the epic flow of history. It would take a long time to list the world-famous (though seldom read) expansive works of epic poetry. In the recitation of hexameter, the triple lifting and sinking of the line must be promoted through breathing that is strong and calm but also urgent. But even shorter poems, hymns and chorales are full of ethical suggestions and high points of the human spirit. They lend themselves well to a convivially instructive recitation. Offered together with similar poems as a *lesson*, they exercise the intellect's [Geist] ability to make insights and recognise contexts.

Great Hymn of Thanksgiving

1

Worship the night and the darkness by which you're surrounded!
Come with a shove
Look at the heavens above:
Day is already confounded.

5

Worship the cold and the dark and calamity dire!
Scan the whole earth:
You're a thing of no worth
And you may calmly expire.

Answers to Questions from the Audience

The Beginning of a Production
On the first day the director introduces his conception of the play and defends it. Along with the actor's materials (a collection mainly of secondary literature) the actor is also burdened with historical information (or what the director takes as such) about fashion and morality, fighting methods and culture during the time of the play, the author's time and the director's time. Luckily,

as the actor realises with relief, this information will barely be used during the course of rehearsals.

Rehearsals

For us there are no reading rehearsals; we go straight into the regular rehearsals. The length of the total rehearsal time varies, but is never less than three months. Right now my wife Barbara and I are staging Brecht's adaptation of Marlowe's *Edward II*. We started in January, are taking a few months off because of this tour and the premiere will be on the 18 June. It's a large production, with almost seventy actors in 140 roles – 140 costumes were specially tailored for this production. A play with battles brings with it the problem of choreography, which does not fit well with stage arrangement and makes extreme demands on the actors. However, battle scenes can produce great special effects, although they must always be appropriate to the intention of the production.

Developing the Role

It is not easy to enter rehearsal and forget experiences that have been successful. Yet you must begin rehearsal like a newborn babe (after extensive preparation and having memorised the text), so that growth in the role has a chance and development is assured. Successful actors are quickly typecast: the working-class type becomes as much of a cliché that can be called up at will as the dangerous and charming Mack the Knife. Sometimes much energy and time must be invested to dismantle the scaffolding of earlier roles (which appear to be so promising and keep on suggesting solutions until they stick like burrs to cloth), before you have created the empty space upon which a new role can be constructed with its own appropriate means.

Example: Cleaning Weapons

In Becher's *Winter Battle* there is a scene in which two friends, German soldiers on the Russian Front, are questioning the very meaning of their situation. In the process their friendship hangs in the balance because the older one, Nohl, decides to desert, while Hörder, whom I played, wants to continue to fight. The director wanted an intense verbal exchange, which was to be emphasised at certain points by me moving towards Nohl whenever I wanted to change his opinion, and him turning and moving away each time he rejected my arguments. It was a constant back-and-forth, coming-and-going – nervous and frenzied but not serious and crucial. Circumstances led to the director's departure and Brecht took over. The first thing he did was to give us a physical action for the scene, an activity that was relevant to the story. What do two soldiers on the Eastern Front do between battles, when not reading, writing letters or sleeping? They clean the weapons that they depend on. Brecht had us sit next to each other and the main action became the cleaning of the machine-guns. We took them apart, rubbed them down with cloths, oiled them and reassembled them, an action that demanded our concentration. Our dialogue, or conflict, was not allowed to interrupt the action yet had to be continued, for it was urgent and could not be postponed. It became quieter, quite incidentally. There was no rush; rather, it faltered. The pauses were dictated by the cleaning of the weapons. It became a very light conversation that ended with Nohl's departure, a final decision when his weapon had been reassembled and was ready to shoot again. The ruptured friendship was not indicated or emphasised through emotions. Nohl's expected exit was used simply: the older comrade, finishing first with his work, stands up and leaves. The end.

Example: Mending Nets

Certain activities or work processes on the stage that are relevant to the play (which is not the case with all of them) should be executed precisely. Weigel learned Carrar's mending of the nets, the family's livelihood, directly from fisherman. Mending nets and baking bread, she carried the conflict calmly and with poise through the entire action, suffering her sons' and visitors' irritability. Finally she takes her gun along with the freshly baked bread and wraps them both as provisions in a piece of cloth. In this way the forced upheaval at the end is both tragic and heroic, but also self-evident.

Audience

In the GDR, there are 157 Brecht and Weigel brigades. Their members have been recognised with these names and have accepted them. They maintain contact with the Berliner Ensemble and the Brecht Archive. The theatre also has connections to the People's Enterprise [VEB] Chemische Werke Buna, to air and naval military forces, and to the Universities of Leipzig, Jena, Dresden and other institutions. Special performances for students and groups of apprentices are organised and they are brought to the theatre in special trains. One group from Jena travelled home at night after a Monday-evening performance in order to continue studying the next morning – a sacrifice for art. Due to audience demand, conversations in the foyer are planned for after each performance, although for my part I don't think much of them, especially after difficult performances. For a while, they were scheduled too often, almost every day. There wasn't always real interest on the part of the audience and the conversations took on a routine character. The main criterion for a successful performance is always the audience – without an audience, even performances that seem great shouldn't be assumed to be so.

Acting as Process

Running productions, even successful ones, are still subject to change and critique. During our production of *Coriolanus*, Brecht's adaptation of Shakespeare's tragedy (which has been handled in the German critical and theatrical traditions as a tragedy of pride) we tried to reduce the lofty claims of the interpretative tradition to an investigation of the seeming irreplaceability of Coriolanus. In this way problems associated with Stalin's cult of personality could be conceptualised and judged differently. In our performance Coriolanus' irreplaceability comes into question and in the end is proved to be illusory. Year after year, the plunge into nothingness just didn't come off right. We noticed this, and discussed it with audiences and colleagues in the theatre. Peter Brook referred us back to Shakespeare, to everything that had to do with the relationship between Volumnia and Coriolanus, and to a certain extent between mother and child. After conferring with him, we took Volumnia's petition of Coriolanus much more seriously, and played out the psychological implications of Coriolanus' break with his own flesh and blood more vehemently. Shakespeare had asserted himself against Brecht's cuts and our simplified conception of the piece. You also shouldn't deny it to yourself when parts of the performance just last too long. Even when you're really in love with a particular scene, you might have to cut it. You have to view the performance as a work in progress that extends beyond a single evening.

BRUFORD SEMINAR LONDON 1981

On the occasion of a series of evening Brecht recitals that took me from Edinburgh to London via a few other cities, the director of a college with a drama department wrote to me requesting that I answer questions from teachers, students and others concerning my experiences in and opinions about the theatre. Because my stays in Great Britain counted (and still count) among the most pleasant that I have experienced, I was happy to agree.

Questions and Answers

Also participating: Barbara Brecht-Schall

QUESTION Would you still describe the Berliner Ensemble as revolutionary theatre? What makes for revolutionary directorial politics?
ES   That's such a lofty term: revolutionary theatre. You could call theatre that takes place during a revolutionary process, which is part of or attaches itself to such a process, revolutionary. That would be theatre performed by actors who are revolutionaries outside the theatre as well, which would mean that there really was a revolution, a social revolution driven on from below, that shots were exchanged with an armed enemy. Jörg Ratgeb, a painter who fought on the side of the farmers during the Peasant Wars, was taken prisoner and quartered. The painter Gustave Courbet, who participated in the uprising of the Paris commune and the destruction of the Vendôme column, was subject to

reprisals later in his life. The writer Ernst Toller was the head of the Bavarian Soldiers' and Workers' Council, and was sentenced to five years in prison after the fall of the Bavarian Soviet. The actor and singer Ernst Busch fought in the Spanish Civil War on the side of the Republic and was then extradited from France, where he had fled, to Germany, where he was sentenced to seven years' hard labour. These men were revolutionaries and at the same time revolutionary artists – because I assume that they wanted not only to improve the people's calamitous social position, but also wished to defend the production of their own art. As far as the Berliner Ensemble is concerned, we stand out because of revolutionary themes, and our plays and productions that put these themes to use. Brecht's instructions, suggestions and references to classics of philosophy (especially to the philosophy of dialectical materialism by writers like Lenin and Mao) offer new ways of seeing both drama and reality. In our own way, we participate in the class struggle raging worldwide that makes itself felt in Europe through the pressure that the two superpowers exert against each other.

Let's put it this way: we're part of a worldwide revolutionary process. In this we're not alone. The masterworks of Soviet revolutionary theatre and film (we know them under this official rubric) thrived not just on the breath of bloody conflict, but also from their consciousness of victory in the civil war and over the intervention – take, for example, Stanislavsky's production of Ivanov's *Armoured Train 14–69* in 1927 or Eisenstein's *Storm over Asia* from 1927. Or Gorky's 1907 novel *The Mother*, dealing with the revolutionary events of 1905, which was adapted by Pudovkin, premiered in 1926, then adapted again by Brecht and premiered in 1932. Even agitprop theatre doesn't necessarily have to be revolutionary (although it seems perfectly suited to this purpose due to its mobile nature and the small, quick forms it uses); it can be employed by the party or the union [*Gewerkschaft*] for political education [*zur linken Aufklärung*], for the purpose of preparation of or debriefing on an action in the everyday class struggle.

53

I cannot accept the term 'directorial politics'. Direction of a play is an artistic undertaking. However, a director's work environment (like an actor's) should be influenced or aided by politics. In the best-case scenario, the effect of a production should also be political, in that it addresses contemporary thought and problems. If you think that the Berliner Ensemble seems different today from thirty years ago when Brecht was alive, you're correct. Attacks, successes, accusations, friendships and animosities accumulate just like back then, but have conformed to the changing times. Every crisis is styled as a final downfall, much in the way that Brecht was damned and failure shrilly prophesied for his theatre every time he produced something weaker than normal. Theatres are subject to fluctuations and changes, and a theatre with an international reputation can't defend its reputation successfully in every production. Jealous people are quick to avenge themselves for the praise that they once had to grant begrudgingly.

QUESTION Does your approach as an actor to a Brecht role differ from your approach to another role?

ES   In and of itself, no. Before I accept or intend to play a role of any kind, my approach is always the same, insofar as it is always different. I'm interested in a role not only from the perspective of an actor, but also as a dramaturg, connoisseur of literature and a politically engaged person with an interest in society. This means that I find certain types of dramatic literature less interesting, or not interesting at all.

QUESTION Is there someone at the Berliner Ensemble who is responsible for the actors' voice and movement training?

ES   We have physical training twice a week. You can also sign up for voice lessons and breathing exercises as often as needed. Unfortunately, this training is not mandatory, which means that attendance is especially low for the physical training, since most actors are terribly lazy when it comes to maintaining the fundaments of their profession. Pure acting instruction, that is, dramatic instruction, does not take place in our theatre; we learn this subject matter in rehearsals.

QUESTION How do you approach a new role?

ES   At the beginning of a new assignment, the interest I have in the play and in my figure is of primary importance. But at the beginning I am not so much interested in representing the dramatic figure as in the philosophical and human problem offered by the play. That is to say, the problem must concern me personally and at the same time be present in the outside world. The problem's societal solution should be related to my personal one; they should be variants of the same effort, striving for conformity. Of course, all art is fiction, merely the assumption of truth and reality, but we forget that completely in the practice of our profession, and gladly. In the time before the rehearsals it's fun to expand your knowledge by reading secondary literature. When I was working on Coriolanus, I took great pleasure in reading more extensively about Roman history during the time of the play and far beyond it. I read histories by Livy, Gibbon and Mommsen, I read Plutarch's forty-six parallel biographies of great Greek and Roman men, in which a Greek and a Roman are always juxtaposed for comparison – in this case, I was especially interested in Coriolanus and Alcibiades. I read critiques about Adalbert Matkowski's famous performance, as well as all sorts of different descriptions of the topic throughout the ages. When you prepare for a role, you read everything that you had previously skimmed and you get closer to the things that you want to use. You necessarily read with more purpose than when you're reading for enjoyment, and you approach an earlier time and culture – not one that is foreign, but merely different, something that you can make use of. The same is true for modern pieces, whether they deal with fascism, socialism or other more narrowly conceived social conditions.

At the beginning of rehearsals all the knowledge you've saved up must be integrated into your being, appearing to have been forgotten. It has to work independently from within you, so that you can go about your work creatively and unencumbered. I think it's good to learn your lines in advance, but there are colleagues of mine who don't do this. But it's important to me because I personally can't just learn phrases; rather, I learn the circumstances of a situation at the same time as the text. I also draft for myself a topography of the spaces in which I will move. Not, however, so that I feel comfortable in them, but rather so as to have an idea of how I can move forwards and backwards logically during the action. I also start to have realisations that of course I can't allow to become fixed while I'm learning; everything must remain unfinished and await completion. When rehearsals begin, memorised text is a double-edged sword; it is a blessing and a curse. You have to be open to the rehearsal process and stay open during rehearsals, so that you can find dramatic ideas or even make new discoveries. Everyone involved has to keep an open mind. Openness is based on trust, which is very important to earn. An actor's thought on stage is thought that is expressed. What you're thinking or feeling up here is unimportant. No one cares. You have to find the outward expression for the thought that you want to convey.

Helene Weigel told me the following story: as a young actress, she appeared alongside the great Albert Bassermann in a 1925 production of Isben's *Pillars of Society*. In one scene during which she was also on the stage, Bassermann received one catastrophic message after another: father dead, mother dead, children dead – all out of nowhere. Bassermann chose a position with his back to the audience when he received these reports of catastrophe. And Helli took him to task one day because he kept his face (which was pointed away from the audience) not only expressionless, but also made private gestures with it, going so far as to wink at her. He supposedly said: who cares. The audience can't see my face. He acted completely and totally with his back, and only there. Every blow that was struck he parried with his back. Bassermann showed how his back contorted and trembled, and that got under people's skin. You have to know how to express something and with what. In art, the 'how' is more important than the 'what'. There are thousands of pictures of the Madonna, but the one by Raphael really touches your heart. So: an actor's thought is thought that is expressed, and not one iota more.

I can also relate a story involving me that happened decades after the Bassermann affair: Weigel was playing my mother (as she often did) in Brecht's production of *Señora Carrar's Rifles*. At the end of the play she limped towards me slowly, a broken woman, away from her eldest son Juan, who had been shot by Franco's henchmen and lay dead on the stage. She knew herself to be guilty for his death. I stood behind her at a window that looked out on to the sea. She came towards me, whom, like Juan, she had forbidden to fight, and pushed herself with her last bit of strength against me, barely able to stand. Before she turned around to say 'Take the guns!' and break with the past, she gasped 'handkerchief!' in a barely audible tone, her back still to the audience, her body pressed closely to mine. I gave her a handkerchief; she blew her nose violently into it and handed it back to me, all without disturbing the play or her performance in the slightest way.

I saw Galina Ulanova as *prima ballerina assoluta* at the Bolshoi Opera in the ballet *Romeo and Juliet* by Prokofiev. Fixed in my memory is the way that she floated towards her dead lover and knelt before him, bending over his body slightly, her bare back rising and falling. Then she danced only with her shoulder blades, expressing a pain that was transferred to every single spectator.

When the actor nears the performance, when he is able to move more easily within the play, his reactions will become faster and more certain. The goal is to be able to turn off the brain, to make all reactions reflexive, automatic. The entire performance should be carried by reflexes: speech, screams, looks, leaps, steps, sleep and silence all must become reflexive. The best acting starts with an intelligent acquisition of the material and moves towards a correct, convincing, but more than anything reflexive performance.

QUESTION Once you've logically worked through the intellectual aspect of your work, how do you get rid of that aspect again in order to move to the reflexive level?

ES   Through practice. You don't act the entire scene by yourself. It is the product of the ensemble (even in a solo performance: you have to multiply yourself into an ensemble). I think that everything you do in a scene should never be thought of as an action, but rather as a reaction. Or, to put it more clearly: everything that you do on stage is a reaction, or it doesn't belong there. You always have to look for the causes or triggers of a situation. You can find them in your partner or partners on stage, in the plot or in the situation itself, but at the beginning you should look for them in the problem posed by the play, the singular guiding spirit of the dramatic work. Your search for causes must always be relevant to the problem of the play. And if you really immerse yourself in the information that is offered to you by the play itself, and don't try to act independently or in an original way, you'll find (after much repetition, admittedly) that your acting will become reflexive.

QUESTION   More reflexive than reactive?

ES   A reflex is a reaction. Reactions drive the plot or the conflict; reflexes are an important component of a naked, immediate performance that has become unpolemical once again.

Please let me also discuss a subject that I hold dear: the autonomous and self-contained nature of a work of art. When Brecht claims in *The Messingkauf Dialogues* (which I mentioned before) that incidents can only be explained through other incidents, he means that nothing should happen in the play that doesn't have a cause within the play and that nothing external to the play should be assumed. Every work of art, whether it is a painting, a sculpture, a piece of music or in our case a theatre production, must be a self-contained universe. Any explanation external to it is meaningless. This was one of the difficulties of Socialist Realism, when it was wrongly understood and became dogma.

For example, you always played Stalin with the requisite greatness; he had to be great, even if he was just looking out of the window. I've played Lenin, Hitler/Ui, Oppenheimer and Galileo, all of whom are historical figures, all of whose positive or negative characteristics don't concern me when I'm first looking for a basis for my acting. I have to approach them during the play, during my preparation, but how? 'Objectively' would not be the correct answer, rather entirely false. I use the technique of subjective defence through their reactions. I defend them as subjects in that I allow them their personal reactions. These reactions become objective actions when they are applied to other people, provoking new reactions in turn. Only then do they become assessable and worthy of critique as social factors.

As an actor, I can't say from the beginning: Richard III is an evil person. That would be an irresponsible claim. Then I wouldn't even need to put on the play. I also shouldn't let it make up the tenor of my portrayal, because the play as a whole will make the truth known, not my individual acting. By the way, were I to make such a premature judgement, I would lose the fun and adventure that are part and parcel of artistic work. I shouldn't approach or play a role with pre-existing notions of a fixed morality or character in mind. On the contrary, I should make an effort to be disinterested. Such judgements should be made in retrospect; the audience can puzzle things over after the play. A production is open, just like the world-historical events to which it is indebted.

What I think or believe privately can be totally different. My job is to play a figure in the play and to leave the judgement to history (represented by the people present). World history, contemporary history and national history [*Geschichte der Völker*] on the one hand and story, plot and a sequence of incidents on the other hand are interchangeable terms to us when we're working on a play. We view them as interchangeable, that is, as far as the essential part of our acting is concerned. To put it as a truism: a pig is a pig, not because it is a pig, but because it acts like a pig. The same is true for heroes.

QUESTION Would you, as a director who works with young actors, require that an actor be familiar with dialectical materialism as it is taught, I believe, in GDR schools, when performing, for example,

'The Song of the Class Enemy', which is contained in your programme?

ES   I would not advise any actor, even an actor from the GDR, to recite this poem or any other poem with a communist perspective unless he sympathises with the standpoint and utopian aspirations of communism. Why should he? Why should he recite or sing 'The Song of the Class Enemy' if he doesn't believe that there's really a class struggle, or if he stands on the other side of the barricades? In order to prove that Brecht was wrong? To make fun of the song? There are enough other poems out there, beautiful ones. However, if you want to recite this poem in good faith you should do it and not study materialist dialectics just for that purpose. I personally am very dependent on the honesty [*Aufrichtigkeit*] of the text that I perform. Once, for an evening recital of Brecht works, I selected 'The Ballad of Mazeppa'. I envisioned Mazeppa as a revolutionary type, one whom the bloodthirsty ruler and his thugs had sworn to kill.

1

They took him and tied him with rope to his stallion
He was bound on his back to the back of his beast
In the darkening evening they drove him out quickly
With a whinnying wild shriek as his steed was released.

For eleven strophes, the poem describes his painful death.

11

Three days he had ridden through morning and evening
Till he reached the age where all pain is suppressed
And then he passed into the great haven of safety
Dead tired he rode on into infinite rest.

In the poem, Brecht doesn't disclose or even allude to the reason that the man was condemned to death. I assumed it was because of a good deed on his part, and recited the poem with seriousness and despair. I empathised with and suffered through the 'three times eternity', the 'three days he rode, with his ropes ever tightening'. Nowhere in any editions of the poem did I find a commentary, but in *Meyers Konversationslexikon* I read:

> Mazeppa, Ivan Stepanovich, Cossack hetman . . . came from Poland to Warsaw to work as a page in the court of King Jan Kazimierz. After being caught in a compromising situation with a baron's wife in 1663, he was bound naked to the back of his own horse, which was then set free and carried him to the Ukraine, where he joined the ranks of the Cossacks after recovering from grievous injuries. [Band 12]

Not a word about death and noble goals. I felt deliberately betrayed by the poet, and didn't want to recite the poem any more. For me, it had been robbed of its content, without which I could not believably recite it.

QUESTION   I worked at the National Theatre, together with Manfred Wekwerth and Joachim Tenschert, on Shakespeare's *Coriolanus*. The production wasn't well received. Do you think this was because of the Berliner Ensemble's attempt to produce a Shakespeare play in a Brechtian manner? In your opinion, should you have put on Brecht's *Coriolanus* instead of Shakespeare's?

ES   I didn't see that production, so I don't know where those particular problems came from. When you produce Shakespeare's tragedies (we're going to produce them soon and I'd love to participate), you of course have to accept Shakespeare's 'maniacs', [*Amokläufer*] as Brecht called them, for what they are. You can't reduce them to normal proportions, to normal people. You have to leave them to their outsized renaissance greatness and conse-quence. I believe, nevertheless, that if I were to play Shakespeare's Coriolanus (and I've played Brecht's hundreds of times) and were to give Shakespeare his due, that Shakespeare, that is to say the text, would not resist my approach. I wouldn't see any insur-mountable difficulty in departing with what bourgeois literary criticism calls 'the tragedy of pride', in seeing Coriolanus as essentially noble not only in comparison to the plebeians, but also to the patricians, indeed, to all levels of society. And this not only because of his noble birth. But this assumption is not important to me. It would also not especially interest me if you could read Shakespeare's play in the same way. I would examine the extent to which Coriolanus differentiates his pride over his own kind from his pride over the others. I would also examine the extent to which his dependence on his mother is a true dependence or a false one. The story between Volumnia and Coriolanus is usually played purely: with a great maternal, protective, guiding love on one side and a great childlike love in need of protection and guidance on the other. You could discover that she is a horrible woman who nurtures his pride and pushes him back into himself. And more than anything else, she is the one who judges him, when the Roman people are no longer able to do so. In the theatre, the grand, pure emotions should be ignored. In any role by any author I would try to determine the conflicts socially and de-emphasise emotional aspects by subjecting them to real scrutiny. As real emotions – that is, as types of behaviour – they become significant again in a different way. This is nothing new, but unfortunately something that has to be proven over and over again.

BBS   In our theatre Helene Weigel played Volumnia and I know that she was thinking about that great photo of the three 'Gold Star Mothers' while she prepared for her role. I don't know if you know what the 'Gold Star' meant in the USA during the Second World War: any mother who had lost more than two sons was allowed to hang a gold star in her window. The photo in question shows three mothers in floral hats proudly receiving congratulations for having sacrificed so much for their country. That's how she wanted to play Volumnia. She would've really liked to wear a floral hat.

ES   But tell everyone that she didn't want to make it into a caricature.

BBS   It wasn't meant as a caricature!

ES   Her love for her son remains unscathed and must remain unscathed.

BBS   That's true – but for us, it's an unusual type of love.

QUESTION   To what extent do you take into account Brecht's writings on dramatic technique, methods and approaches to productions, the *Verfremdungseffekt*, etc., during day-to-day work at the Berliner Ensemble?

ES   The important members of the Ensemble don't have to consult those writings like the Bible; some of it is in their flesh and blood. I wouldn't know how to prevent myself, while learning a piece, from continually revising a list of the strengths and weaknesses of each figure, in order to let justice and injustice be correctly articulated. I wouldn't know how to stop myself from being concerned with focusing the problem, with articulating the normal, with translating what I want to express into an understandable *Gestus* that is at once noticeable and creates a simple stance. The word *Verfremdungseffekt* just came up again. The *Verfremdungseffekt* is really only a secondary element, but of course an effective one. It is not the method, but a means of the method, a technical aid and an ancient one at that, one which Brecht did not invent. Every comic uses it; Immanuel Kant described it accurately. Brecht only tried to adapt it to a new purpose.

QUESTION   Can you demonstrate what the *Verfremdungseffekt* means to an actor?

ES   *Verfremdung* means nothing other than opening up a thing or a process to a newly aroused attentiveness. It is an attempt to find points in a play that go unnoticed in normal life due to habit, even though they are disgusting, horrible, or laughable, or because they are actually admirable, endearing or heroic. If you want to stress such a neglected point, you must act in a way that the audience – expecting something familiar to be normal – is not disappointed but rather irritated, wondering: Wait? What's this? According to Immanuel Kant in his *Anthropology*, it

> . . . rouses the mind to collect its thoughts for reflection; it is the
> stimulus to *astonishment* (which already involves reflection). . . . it is
> the role of art to represent ordinary things from an aspect that

makes them striking. [Kant, *Anthropology from a Pragmatic Point of View*, trans. Mary J. Gregor]

Eventually the audience or observer is supposed to reach an insight. That was a new view on a point of reality. Brecht emphasises in *The Messingkauf Dialogues* that 'social interactions can be labelled . . . as something that calls for explanation . . . not just as something natural'. He denies the naturalness of certain kinds of interpersonal relationships and defines them as impoverished; they lack the self-reflective thought which goes beyond themselves and activates the people in question. It is inconsequential thinking that Brecht is criticising. In the twelfth scene of *Saint Joan of the Stockyards*, during which Johanna dies and is canonised, she recognises:

> It makes no sense to say there's something deep inside of you that
> won't come out! Can you think of anything
> That has no consequences? . . .
> Oh inconsequential goodness! Oh negligible virtue!

In his poem 'To the Germans' Friedrich Hölderlin writes accusatorially:

> Never laugh at the child who with his whip and spurs
>   On his horse made of wood deems himself bold and great,
>   For you, Germans, you too are
>   Poor in deeds and with fancies filled.
> [*Hölderlin. His Poems*, trans. Michael Hamburger]

Brecht hoped to give his theatre visitors the ability to 'criticise constructively from a social point of view'.

I must admit, however, that the possibility of insight hardly results in necessary actions being taken.

BBS Take Volumnia, with this maternal love, this all-encompassing maternal love. If you assume this is something natural, then you have to show how unnatural this natural thing can be, this love for her son that leads to his death.

ES   Basically, the *Verfremdungseffekt* is really just the representation of a contradiction, a contradiction in society, a contradiction
between subjectivity and the assumption of a final, real stance
towards reality. Brecht's Galileo did not interest me as great
physicist. He's someone who employs reason and has fun doing it,
someone who uses reason like a tool, like a lever. Throughout the
entire play he says things that express his opinion about reason. In
the third scene he says to his friend Sagredo: 'Yes, I believe in
reason's gentle tyranny over people.' That is at the beginning of
the play. He hasn't yet been shaken by reality. That quote is
beautiful, is it not? You wouldn't mind signing your name to it. But
I think it is important for the figure of Galileo to speak this line as
if it is false. How do I do it? I speak superficially, without conviction. [Demonstrated during the seminar.] Then the spectators
say to themselves: such a beautiful line, such a beautiful, profound
thought, and he says it like that. And that's what I aim to achieve.
In the last scene Galileo says to Andrea: 'Reason is something
people can be divided into. It can be described as the egoism of all
humanity. Such egoism is not strong enough.' His change of
opinion is his downfall. Therefore, I wouldn't think it right to let
the wisdom of old age to speak here (which would, no doubt, be
well received). Instead, a man who has given up the fight speaks
about his hopeless position, about something that no longer
concerns him. I think that could be stimulating for some audiences
as well. Acts based on reason are often the result of an individual's
relationship to authority and reality. *Verfremdung* is simple. The
only prerequisite is that you have your own opinion, and take care
that it doesn't get lost in the play's message and the opinions of the
other actors. We can distance [*verfremden*] things through the most
diverse means. The acting can be distanced by the costumes, like
in animal fables, or the acting can distance the costumes. When
you've recognised or agreed upon a scene's main contradiction,
you can distance it through the element(s) you find most effective:
acting and set, scene and songs – but the best means of *Verfremdung*
remain those which pull the contradiction out of a performance's

unity. Basically, every stylistic change, all eclecticism is *Verfremdung*. Just like in Shakespeare, when the verse breaks off and the prose begins. The actors have to make sure the spectators notice: Do you hear? Now we're speaking in prose, and as of now, in verse again. The audience becomes alert and can consider: why the difference?

BBS That's right. If you intend to disrupt, you have to do it seriously.

QUESTION I don't know what kind of audiences you have in your country, or how large they are, but our audiences here make up just a small minority of the population. Given this context, what kind of role can theatre play?

ES We have the luck that our theatre is usually full. In our country, the GDR, we have over sixty theatres with permanent ensembles, which issue year-long contracts to their actors and other employees. There are theatres that are extremely busy and those that are less busy. What can the theatre achieve? Well, I don't think that it can achieve very much. It's enough for me if I can get a few people to think differently, get them to listen to what I have to say through my roles. I want to convey little things, and I've ascertained that, now and again, I do convey something. I personally didn't join the theatre to change society. I was an exhibitionist. I wanted to publicly express myself, to lose myself. I was much too uncontrolled to show more than my own helplessness, much too stupid to wish for anything more. Only later did I face the unpleasant task of having to justify my career choice to myself, to defend it against my own misgivings.

QUESTION Brecht revised scenes continuously during rehearsals. When you put on plays by Brecht today, do you also edit or partially revise them as you see fit?

ES No, you shouldn't write any new texts, even though Brecht answers the question 'Can we amend Shakespeare?' in 'A Study of Shakespeare's *Coriolanus*' by saying, I think we can amend Shakespeare if we can amend him.' Rewriting texts should not become fashionable. If you want something that the play doesn't offer you should write another play, if you are able. Of course, you can change the play from a dramaturgical standpoint and create a concept for the production. This concept should not be directly hostile to the play and wish to undermine it, however. You can leave out scenes, change their position in the play or make cuts.

QUESTION Concerning the question of changes – I participated in the first production of *Mother Courage*. A director, Carl Maria Weber, was officially assigned to us for the purpose of overseeing the production. He insisted that everything be exactly the same as it was at the Berliner Ensemble.

ES What a terrible idea. Absurd. A description of a production pre-recorded in a model book [*Modellbuch*] can help save you some work – you don't have to reinvent the wheel. But it's not a requirement and certainly not dogma. Naturally you have to go beyond it, deviate from it. Or you can put it aside entirely.

QUESTION I'd like to know if the current production's set design is different from previous ones – the play is still on the theatre schedule.

BBS It's not 'still' on the theatre schedule, it's there again. It's a new production. The set design is now different.

ES At the Berliner Ensemble, there have been several plays put on several times, many by different directors. I've already played some roles that I got to know or informed myself about with the help of other actors. In the case of Galileo, I read about Charles Laughton's portrayal and saw it in an amateur film. I played both Andreas and the ballad singer to Ernst Busch's Galileo. I played Cardinal Barberini, who later becomes pope, to Wolfgang Heinz's Galileo. I knew how they played him and had my own opinions about it, had my own motivation for playing Galileo myself. If I play him differently from the others, it should be seen as proof of the work I have put into the role, not as my desire to be original or confrontational.

QUESTION Concerning the excerpt from *The Trial of Lucullus*, which was part of the programme, I would like to ask Mr Schall if he sees Brecht's and Dessau's operas as operas or as theatrical works. Does he think that operatic forms derived from Brecht/ Dessau make sense and is the opera viable as a form?

ES *Lucullus* and *Puntilla* by Brecht and Dessau are most definitely operas, and cannot be put on (by which I mean sung more than anything) by actors. I played Lucullus in the radio play, which was written before the opera. He was a really strong character. And for the recording of the opera I played the court crier. The *Sprechgesang* [speech-song] in the 'Song of the Fishwife' (included in my programme) doesn't provide me with any difficulties. In performing it I wanted to assume a human stance and make it clear that it actually doesn't matter if it is performed by a male or a female figure. I can take on certain female stances without trying to be a woman – I act like a man trying to act like a woman. When the tyranny of gender falls away, behaviours and emotions become more social [*gesellschaftlicher*], actually personal.

QUESTION Could Herr Schall explain (or, even better, demonstrate) what *Gestus* or gestural acting means?

ES *Gestus* is behaviour depicted on stage – a mixture of feeling and reaction, an activity in the broadest sense. The meaning of the *Gestus* takes precedence over the verbal meaning of the text. In this way you can express every sentence in the most diverse ways, even ways contrary to the meaning of the sentence. You can say the word 'no' with the *Gestus* 'no', but a girl who is asked 'Do you love me?' and doesn't have the nerve to say yes, says no in this way: [Demonstrated during the seminar.] That's not a 'no' any more, rather half of a 'yes'. That's *Gestus*. You can say it spiritedly: [Demonstrated during the seminar.] Or you say it with contempt: [Demonstrated during the seminar.] And you've turned it into its opposite. Every sentence can be varied or turned into its opposite by taking a stance which guides its sense. In my roles I often choose a warm-up phrase with which I can catapult myself into the scene. I get a better grip on the scene that way. They're usually simple phrases. During Coriolanus' first appearance on stage, he meets the mutinying plebeians.

As Coriolanus in Brecht's Shakespeare adaptation of the same name, 1964. With Hilmar Thate as Aufidius. (photo by Maria Steinfeldt)

MENENIUS (*who has already noticed* CAIUS MARCIUS, *to a plebeian*)
> You scoundrel! Very well, 'no war for Rome'?
> Rome will make war upon its rats. Once and
> For all it will . . . Hail, noble Marcius!

MARCIUS
> Thanks. What's the matter? Got the itch again?
> Scratching your old scabs?

And then he rages on for a page until:

> . . . – they'd get their answer
> From my sword. And with my lance I'd measure
> Not grain but their corpses by the bushel
> In the streets of Rome.
> You fragments. Now inscribe your names in the lists!
> [Translation altered to match the Berliner Ensemble's version]

The text invites a brutish approach from beginning to end. That was exactly what displeased us – at least as far as the first half was concerned. Therefore I remained hesitant, with my sword sheathed, in consternation, stricken by the plebeians' unjust behaviour, the very unexpectedness of which weighed on my heart. Before I went on stage and found myself in the situation of confronting the insubordinate men, I drilled into my head the stance I would take during my first impression of the situation. The sentence was: 'This can't be true, what I'm experiencing here is impossible.' After warming up in this way I began my speech in a controlled manner, almost amiably.

BBS   Now I would like to request that you not ask any more questions. He loves to talk about these things and would continue if he could, but he has to perform later on. And if anyone should say that he's lost his voice this evening, I'm relying on all of you to explain how it happened.

SCUOLA SEMINAR
MILAN 1985

Because of my bond of friendship with Giorgio Strehler I visited his school, where I faced an onslaught of questions and presented my own ideas. He was especially interested in the relationship between Brechtian and Aristotelian theatre.

I assume that you are all students of this theatre school or already actors, so I want to emphasise from the beginning that all good acting is very similar. And since I've been asked to talk specifically about Brechtian theatre, I'd like to add that it too is, in practice, not a big exception, provided it is successful and therefore exceptional, and is compared to other equally successful and exceptional forms of theatre.

When you join the theatre, you should bring at least two different interests with you: first, an interest in acting and second, an interest in reality, in the life all around you. At the beginning of your career these two interests need not necessarily have an immediate connection to aesthetics or ideology. You can deepen your knowledge in these areas later, or ignore them altogether. In the beginning you have to be interested in expressing yourself, however vitally or intelligently. This interest in reality may restrict itself solely to the question: how do people interact? Great acting always strives to convey human suffering or joy; the former makes you sad and empathetic, the latter makes you cheerful and hopeful.

Giorgio Strehler, the director of your school and surely your role model and mentor, published his 'written, spoken and actualised thoughts' as a book titled *Per un Teatro Umano* [*Towards a Human Theatre*]. He did this simply and unspectacularly, without threatening postures or didactic intentions, neither as a know-it-all nor as someone out to settle scores. In the canon of theatres which have variously described themselves as emotional [*einfühlend*], unchained, biomechanical, surrealistic, realistic, expressionistic, political, existential, cruel, absurd, poor, gestural, epic, distancing [*verfremdend*] didactic or dialectical, Strehler's modest claim seems to linger at the end of the list, like a pious wish. But as endearing as his theatre is, as great as it is, he is also passionately interested in liveliness on stage, in interaction. For him, even loneliness is an interpersonal phenomenon, if only within a memory that will not let go of the past.

Consider the end of his production of Carlo Goldoni's *Le Baruffe Chiozzotte*: a figure stands on stage silhouetted by light falling from different angles which reaches the figure but does not fill up the entire space. Crepuscular and calm, the play ends, flowing like a poem by Josef von Eichendorff:

And my soul spread
Its wings out wide,
And flew through the silent regions
As if it were flying home.
[*Great German Poems of the Romantic Era*,trans. Stanley Appelbaum]

And this, after the stage had seethed with everyday life like in narrow Italian alleys, free of tourists, where laughter and poetry echoed, crude and tender. Those wonderful actors performed with luminous (I'll use the word again) poetry, a turbulent lust for life and an infectious lightness. Strehler's understanding of Brecht is also humane and very clever. He asks: *And what is Verfremdung?*

This mysterious matter, epic *Verfremdung*, which no one can fully grasp in reality. But what is *Verfremdung* really other than a 'poetic' procedure? Perhaps the procedure most fundamental to poetry?

The actor 'highlights' something through a particular tone, gesture or both (he has an endless number of possibilities at his disposal), and thereby distances himself from what he is portraying. And at this moment he stops or accelerates time, he transforms it into 'something different'. . . .

[Ungaretti] says something like: Poetry? That's what makes clear things obscure and obscure things clear. And for me, that's exactly what epic distance is, Brecht's *Verfremdung*. It's something that's astoundingly simple on a human level, and only gets complicated because humans have such a rich diversity of possibilities at their disposal. Epic distanciation means giving a concept, idea, or image meaning through one of many other various means. [Giorgio Strehler, *Für ein menschlicheres Theater*, Henschel]

When I talk about the kind of theatre that I make, I mean a theatre influenced not only by Brecht, but by many different people, both famous and lesser known.

I can hardly talk about Aristotle and the theatre without opening myself to the controversy that the young Brecht already started with his predecessors. Brecht's respect for Aristotle's *Poetics* surprised me, as did his careful approach to the work. He agreed with some things and indicated others that he could not accept. He inserted two notes into his personal copy from the *Philosophische Bibliothek* (translated by Alfred Gudeman and published in 1921 by Felix Meiner in Leipzig), and wrote a bit in the book itself. There are also two notes between the table of contents and the translator's introduction.

for contemporary dramatists, aristotle is in no way a dethroned ruler. scholarship [*Wissenschaft*] has yet to truly grasp the actual meaning of his rules, so great is their authority!

and:

I. LESSING rightly held the rules that A. set out in his POETICS to be as infallible as EUCLID'S elements. the authority of both doctrines has extended throughout two centuries and, for certain functions, these rules still have validity. however, like a NON-EUCLIDIAN GEOMETRY, one can and one must set up a NON-ARISTOTELIAN DRAMATURGY.

Brecht's object of criticism here is not Aristotle, but rather the lack of meaning of Aristotle's criteria for Brecht's time, even as he recognises their validity. This fact has probably been forgotten in the meantime. Aristotle writes,

> Epic poetry and tragedy, as also comedy, dithyrambic poetry, and most flute-playing and lyre-playing, [*The Complete Works of Aristotle*, revised Oxford translation, ed. Jonathan Barnes]

Brecht must have done a bit of research, because he wrote over the last three words 'flute and guitar', in a tiny and almost illegible hand,

> are all, viewed as a whole, modes of imitation, [Ibid.]

and Brecht writes characteristically:

> chap 1, 2
> an instructive example for the way in which the transformation of artistic forms advances (caused by functional changes within society). the characteristic of imitative representation remains intact, but loses its determining character entirely. because if you call it imitative (and you can, there are plenty of examples to be found) then imitation [*Nachahmung*] comes after reality, but after imitation, nothing else. in imitation, the process of translation reaches its definitive conclusion. to do justice to modern performance, you would have to call it 'pre-mitative' [*Vorahmung*].

Aristotle surely accommodated Brecht in noting that 'according to some, . . . plays [are] termed dramas, because in a play the personages act the story'. Imitation appealed to both of them:

> . . . Imitation is natural to man from childhood, one of his advantages over the lower animals being this, that he is the most imitative creature in the world, and learns at first by imitation. And it is also natural for all to delight in works of imitation. The truth of

this second point is shown by experience: though the objects themselves may be painful to see, we delight to view the most realistic representations of them in art, the forms for example of the lowest animals and of dead bodies. [*Aristotle*, ibid.]

Films and TV programmes are the first things that occur to me in this context.

The explanation is to be found in a further fact: to be learning something is the greatest of pleasures not only to the philosopher but also to the rest of mankind, however small their capacity for it. [Ibid.]

After this almost cheerful lecture by the wise man of the ancient world, Brecht's remarks seem to me both bitterly serious and pointedly sarcastic:

IV, I
from the beginning, imitation is taken for an aesthetic phenomenon. in any case its purposes do not concern aesthetics.

It's interesting how Brecht rewrites this thesis so succinctly.

humans acquire knowledge through imitation. their 'first', great pleasure comes from learning, that is: the pleasure of learning and the pleasure of imitation are one and the same; however, thereafter the knowledge disappears from their field of vision and pleasure appears, just like in procreation, when the pleasure comes from the friction instead of from the children, from the act of imitation itself, and not from the mastery of what is being imitated.

The older Brecht starts to emerge here clearly – and we have to tell him that he hasn't changed very much, even if he should answer with an 'Oh!' and turn pale, just like his Herr K. Even when Aristotle talked about how the tragedy went through many changes, gradually reached maturity, was perfected and then stopped developing on 'its attaining to its natural form'. Brecht writes polemically on the margins (I was finally able to decipher his handwriting): 'because its basic social function no longer changed'.

I've observed a specific type of process at work in our theatres over the past few decades – one that is opposite to the tragedy's development during the time of the genre's great writers, whom Aristotle describes:

> The number of actors was first increased to two by Aeschylus, who curtailed the business of the Chorus, and made the dialogue take the leading part in the play. A third actor and scenery were due to Sophocles. [*Aristotle*, ibid.]

Today directors are proud of producing tragedies with fewer and fewer actors and less and less scenery (and not only for financial reasons). The dialogue is neglected and the choruses are shifted to the foreground, or the choruses are recruited and merely 'furnished' with dialogue. In contrast, strangely enough, the protagonist is often rendered impotent by dividing the titular figure's role among many actors, thus collectivising the main concern of the play in a banal fashion.

I love conclusive definitions:

> A tragedy, then, is the imitation of an action that is serious and also, as having magnitude, complete in itself; in language with pleasurable accessories, each kind brought in separately in the parts of the work; in a dramatic, not in a narrative form; with incidents arousing pity and fear, wherewith to accomplish its catharsis of such emotions. [Ibid.]

According to Aristotle, fear and pity (taking part in pain you have never experienced) form the medium that allows you to leave the theatre refined and innerly purified. With Brecht, empathy is also produced, but without a personal loss that could diminish the losses portrayed on stage. So here are the two fronts: on one side the attempted insight into possible mechanisms caused or activated by describable antagonists, on the other side the impossibility of insight, because the causes and perpetrators of suffering are Gods and fate or entanglements and inevitabilities that run through generations.

Brecht writes in his 'Critique of the *Poetics*', which is a critique of empathy

> We're with Aristotle (in the fourth chapter of the *Poetics*) as long as he talks about the joys of imitative representation and its basis in learning. But already in the sixth chapter he gets more specific and restricts the range of imitation allowed the tragedy. Only actions that arouse fear or pity should be imitated, and the express purpose of imitation must be to cause fear and pity. It becomes apparent that the actor's imitation of people in action should cause the spectators to imitate the actor. The work of art is received by means of empathy with the actor and, by extension, with the figure in the play. [Brecht, GW 15]

We tend towards sympathy, towards empathy with the terrors of other people, because we are inclined to do so as good-natured people ourselves. And we hope that if we feel good when we suffer and cry, nothing will happen to us, that barbarism will pass us over, and, from the place where it rages, deliver us further reasons to feel sympathy, a sympathy that does not condition resistance and requires no weapons.

In the section 'On Rational and Emotional Standpoints' Brecht states something very clearly that many people still don't want to accept even today:

> The disavowal of empathy does not spring from or lead to a disavowal of emotion. It is the duty of non-Aristotelian drama to prove vulgar aesthetics wrong when it claims that emotions can only be triggered by empathy. However, non-Aristotelian drama must subject the emotions that it conditions and embodies to careful critique. [Ibid.]

This is true: neither the actor's nor the audience's sympathy may take the upper hand, otherwise the opposing party, the one who causes suffering, is strengthened in an unnoticeable and powerful way. This is because there is nothing else that the sympathiser can do except to sit still. Feel what you can, that is, whatever you can manage: you have to make this effort – because if you're not able to deal with suffering, to work against it, if need be, you may be made its accomplice in the end, and not in the theatre. No one wants to do without strong emotions, especially after a theatre visit, but they don't last long. They're always endangered by direct and indirect influences, by our rootedness in everyday life, in a reality that does not leave us time to live our emotions. Praise be to those feelings which can assert themselves for a while without being reduced to more modest behaviour through our actions or decisions. How often are our attitudes saturated in lost emotions.

For Aristotle:

> The plot, in our present sense of the term, is simply this, the combination of the incidents[.] [*Aristotle*, ibid.]

And Brecht regrets that:

> Our theatres no longer have the ability or desire to tell these stories clearly (even the great Shakespeare's stories, which aren't so old), to make the chain of events believable. And the plot is, according to Aristotle – we agree on this point – the soul of the drama.

Aristotle's description of plot is so modern that he could have written it today:

> The most important [element of tragedy] is the combination of the incidents of the story. Tragedy is essentially an imitation not of persons but of action and life. All human happiness or misery takes the form of action; the end for which we live is a certain kind of activity, not a quality. Character gives us qualities, but it is in our actions that we are happy or the reverse. In a play accordingly they do not act in order to portray the characters; they include the characters for the sake of the action. So that it is the action in it, i.e. its plot, that is the end and purpose of the tragedy; and the end is everywhere the chief thing. [*Aristotle*, ibid.]

His triumphant conclusion is: 'that the first essential, the life and soul, so to speak, of tragedy is the plot'.

I'm skipping over a lot and want to turn to other things now, but I can't resist quoting the following:

> Of simple plots and actions the episodic are the worst. I call a plot episodic when there is neither probability nor necessity in the sequence of its episodes. [Ibid.]

A figure moves verbally and literally through the disagreements in the chain of events (incidents, happenings), and is a figure insofar as it has a name, character traits (certain assigned qualities) and is at best performed, that is, embodied. It is not a figure by virtue of being part of the plot, which is made of actions, opinions (thoughts through which the speaker tries to prove something or express a general truth) and modes of behaviour that drive events. It only becomes a figure when it impresses the spectator as such; it is a result independent of the actor's intentions.

The plot has to be self-contained, even closed – it must assume nothing outside itself. The same is actually true for any work of art. It must function like clockwork, must represent its own world, cosmos, universe. Movement within the plot, as work of art, is produced by reactions, all incidents comprise reactions. The performance requires no action or explanation as a prerequisite for an event.

In *The Messingkauf Dialogues*, the philosopher explains to the dramaturg:

> Let's take the play *Wallenstein* by the German author Schiller. In it a general betrays his monarch. Instead of the sequence of incidents in the play proving that this betrayal necessarily leads to the traitor's moral and physical destruction, this is assumed from the first. The world can't exist on a basis of treachery, in Schiller's view. Though he does nothing to prove it. And he couldn't prove such a thing, because it would rule the world out. What he suggests is that it wouldn't be pleasant to live in a world like that, where treachery occurred. Not that he proves that either, of course.

Aristotle describes the same thing in this way:

We have laid it down that a tragedy is an imitation of an action that is complete in itself, as a whole of some magnitude; for a whole may be of no magnitude to speak of. Now a whole is that which has beginning, middle, and end. A beginning is that which is not itself necessarily after anything else, and which has naturally something else after it; an end is that which is naturally after something itself, either as its necessary or usual consequent, and with nothing else after it; and a middle, that which is by nature after one thing and has also another after it. A well-constructed plot, therefore, cannot either begin or end at any point one likes; beginning and end in it must be of the forms just described. [*Aristotle*, ibid.]

The folly of socialist realism was to have forbidden this restriction. Up until the last written insert in the *Poetics*, the two opponents remain in accord, although Brecht regrets having to insist on more, that is, on something else.

As a rough general formula, a length which allows of the hero passing by a series of probable or necessary stages from bad fortune to good, or from good to bad, may suffice as a limit for the magnitude of the story. [Ibid.]

Brecht replies:

VII, 3
undergoing a turnabout from bad fortune into good fortune or from good fortune into bad fortune is really enough, if it's a truly emotional business. unfortunately, for the understanding of modern processes, not one 'up' or 'down' but several ups and downs are necessary.

With that, I will say no more about Aristotelian theatre. It remains a temptation that even non-Aristotelian actresses and actors repeatedly and gladly succumb to, as I experienced in my work with the great Helene Weigel.

In order to acquaint myself with a role at the beginning of my work, I usually write something down: the plot of the play, the figure's back story, or abbreviated versions of the two (whereby descriptions of the play and the figure can overlap, as is the case for titular figures), notes on interpretation, relevant thoughts, poems concerning the plot or figure, production correspondence, scene epigraphs, figure descriptions, etc.

Examples:
Plot description:
Coriolanus by William Shakespeare, adapted by Bertolt Brecht
Attempt at a plot summary
Goal: tell the story in such a way as to be able to do without an external formulation of the play's main concern.

I'll take the key scene between mother and son, the 'entreaty' [Bittgang] at the end of the play.
Act V, Scene IV
Coriolanus is losing time in awaiting Rome's unconditional surrender. Tullus Aufidius criticises him for this. Coriolanus is proud of the consistency of his behaviour, which Tullus Aufidius acknowledges. Coriolanus speaks of Menenius' visit, calling him the Romans' last resort. Tullus Aufidius reminds Coriolanus that this old man also begged that Coriolanus sacrifice himself for Rome (with the entreaty: 'Go and hang yourself!'). Aufidius makes it clear that for Coriolanus there are only two choices: bring about the fall of Rome or commit suicide before the Volscians kill him for deserting.

The apex of Coriolanus' consistent, recalcitrant stance is in his rejection of the entreaties of the women of Rome's great families, his mother, wife and young son among them. Coriolanus is certain that he is not the slave of nature or the [Jakob] Geherda of instinct [reference to an early dramatic fragment of Brecht's]. He is certain in his ability to act inhumanly and according to his principles. Coriolanus greets the delegation, especially his family and Valeria, and does not wish to be asked to negotiate with Rome. He announces, for himself and on the part of his allies, that neither he nor they wish to hear a private word from Rome. Volumnia begs

Coriolanus to act compassionately for Rome, to kill himself or let himself be killed. She will meet both possible outcomes of a fight between the Romans and the Volscians (led by Coriolanus) with her own suicide, the guilt for which she now lays on her son's shoulders. Virgilia joins Volumnia in this decision. Coriolanus wants to end the debate. From now on, Volumnia will be publicly ashamed of her son. Volumnia describes to Coriolanus a very different Rome from the one that he left. The mortal danger that he represents for everyone has changed many things. Rome will not surrender. The citizens of Rome will fight.

Note: The situation forces Volumnia to agitate convincingly for the empowerment of the Roman citizens, even if she calls them rabble. The tribune Junius Brutus rightly notes that Volumnia's sort of patriotism leads her to prefer the victory of the Roman citizens (which will bring them rights and recognition), over reaching an agreement with the Volscian nobility. Volumnia denies her son the honour of having a Roman family. Coriolanus is deeply hurt.

Plot description:

Woyzeck by Georg Büchner

What do I want to portray?

Two scenes, one with Woyzeck's comrade, the other with his wife.

3

Woyzeck and the soldier Andres are not on duty. They are cutting sticks for their captain, and Woyzeck is describing the practices of the Freemasons, who, like the Jews during the time of the Nazis, have [seemingly] infested the entire world. Andres sits next to Woyzeck when he sees him begin to tremble once again as a result of the experiment with peas. A sudden fit, expressed as an apocalyptic vision, causes Woyzeck to spring up, trembling with fear, and jerk Andres into a protective bush beside him (this fit, possibly brought about by Woyzeck's restricted diet, has to allow for an eruption of immense hatred for social injustice, the downtrodden man's most extreme wish – the demise and destruction of the circumstances that oppress him). Greatly disturbed by Woyzeck's changed state, Andres (not having heard or seen anything other-worldly or secretive in the earth or in the sky) enquires as to his friend's condition. Everything is in order again, and when they hear a distant beating of the drums, they run to the city with their bundles of sticks.

4

Woyzeck comes running to his wife in order to tell her that he has recognised and seen through the unscrupulous practices of the Freemasons, and is on the trail of others who pose a threat to the world. Through her unsympathetic posture, Marie tries to brush him off as if he were ill. But he draws her attention to reality, which, although oppressive and unexplainable, should be friendly and transparent. Woyzeck is the only one with an explanation, but he knows that it won't do any good – not for him, Marie, or the world. He greets his child briefly (after being reminded to do so by Marie), as he hurries off to a merry rendezvous.

Character description:
A character description is briefer and more tightly constructed.
Alexei in *Optimistic Tragedy* by Vsevolod Vishnevski
Alexei, a revolutionary and sailor in the Baltic fleet, fights on land and water against the Tsar's generals and the German invaders, fully in accord with his comrades. But he is not interested in what will come after victory. He is too caught up in his hatred for the old times, which he sees firmly rooted and undying in the people around him. There is not time enough or sympathy to dig out the small kernel of hope buried in every soldier; therefore many are lost. Alexei learns that dividing lines do not run only between the fronts, but also between people and friendships. Struggling on, he decides to fight for the commissar of the regiment – for the side that she represents and her dreams for the future.

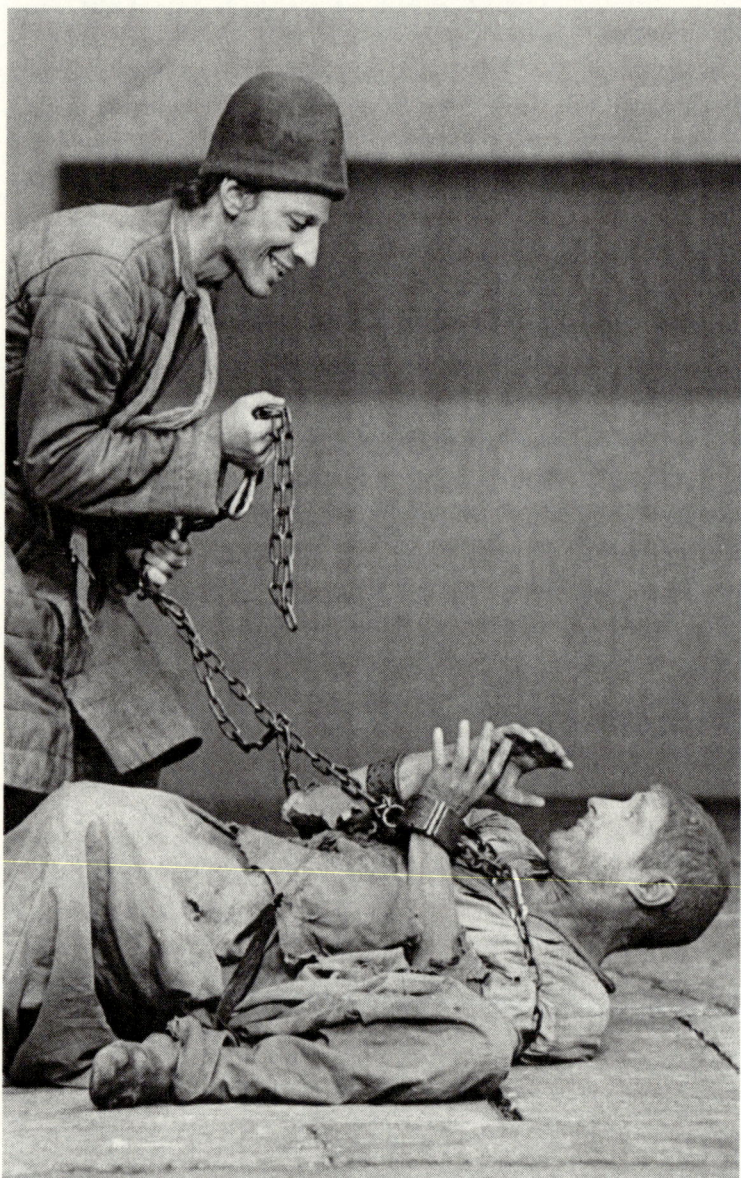

As Azdak in Brecht's Caucasian Chalk Circle *(with Michael Gerber as Shauva), 1976*
(photo by Maria Steinfeldt)

Character description:
The village clerk in *The Causasian Chalk Circle* by Bertolt Brecht
Azdak, the village clerk who anticipates the dawning of a new
age, is shocked on hearing that he has accidentally sheltered the
fleeing Grand Duke. He wishes to anticipate the judgement of
the victorious people and thus has himself brought in chains by
the village policeman from Nuhka, the capital, to Grusinia,
where the weavers' revolt is under way. His expectations come
to naught: the revolt is put down violently. Due to the
uncertainty of the new circumstances, the knights appoint him
judge as a joke. He passes judgement as he sees fit, laden with
disappointment and the need for catching up on life's vulgar (yet
expensive) pleasures. Because he often decides in favour of the
poor and disabled, he is to be hanged when the time of chaos and
disorder is over. But the Grand Duke, whose life Azdak once
saved, returns and pardons him, appointing him once again as
judge. For his first case he must return a child to its proper
mother. He makes a sign to Grusha, the maid, telling her to lie so
that he can give the child to her. She doesn't lie, however, and
this only confirms his embittered opinion of the people. But her
simple nature impresses him, so he arranges a sort of duel
between her and her opponent, the governor's wife, in the
knowledge that Grusha is the stronger of the two due to her
duties as a maid. The victor will be the one to pull the child out
of a chalk circle. Grusha refuses to pull, so as not to hurt the
child. After a second attempt, Azdak recognises the human
greatness contained in Grusha's defeat. He assigns custody of the
child to the maid, the loser, the one who rescued and saved the
child, and denies custody to the biological mother, who
abandoned the helpless child. Then he disappears in order to
escape new personal difficulties.

Short plot description:
Fatzer, in *Demise of the Egoist Johann Fatzer* by Bertolt Brecht,
adapted by Heiner Müller

1. Emancipatory act
2. A step into isolation
3. Beginning of a series of property seizures
4. Fatzer claims leadership and begins to resemble a dictator
5. All of Fatzer's attempts to break out of isolation fail
6. Arrest, condemnation and liquidation of the leader while the emancipatory act is brought to a halt
7. Liquidation of everyone, defeat

A choir entirely of consuming voyeurs.
Meaning of the story in history:
The group of soldiers, posited as a social microcosm, portray the beginning and end of their corresponding macrocosm – of a revolutionary party.

Scene Title:
The Life of Edward II of England by Bertolt Brecht (after Marlowe)
From a production at the Berliner Ensemble by Barbara and me:

1. The king dies – love is victorious – the parliament is in danger
2. Love is costly – the hunt begins
3. A hunting hound is won
4. The prey bares its teeth – the hunting hound smells the bait
5. From too much into nothingness
6. The prey is caught – the hunt is costly
7. Weathervanes show which way the wind is blowing
8. The pause that refreshes
9. Nothingness approaches – cowardice is victorious – the hunting hound trembles
10. Love meets love – the path into nothingness goes forward
11. The pack sniff victory
12. False love arrives – the betrayed pack run amok
13. Nothingness remains at bay
14. The trap snaps closed – the pack become prey
15. Nothingness begins

16. Victory becomes defeat – the hunting hound is released
17. The hunting hound takes the bait – he becomes a wolf
18. The husk lives – the lost victory is paid for – the hunt continues
19. The weathervane turns
20. The prey is caught – the cock crows twice
21. Revenge is sweet – the crown remains on the (at last truly) royal head
22. The weathervane seeks the wind
23. The devastation of war becomes visible
24. A breath of wind
25. The pack turn – the wolf defends itself
26. He said yes [Der Jasager]
27. Waiting
28. He said no [Der Neinsager]
29. The wolf trembles
30. Nothingness here too
31. Nothingness was bought at too dear a price – the pack tear the wolf apart – the king is dead – long live the king

Poetic reflections on plots or characters:
The Prince of Homburg by Heinrich von Kleist
In answer to the play's epigraph:

> If you break the law, don't lay claim to it
> degenerate further, with clenched fists.

On Kleist's play *The Prince of Homburg*:

> It concerns dust. But was it wiped away?
> Why not? It must remain for the enemy.
> And the state, too, is the enemy, lying
> on its own ground, gasping into its lung.
>
> Prince Dust of Homburg, candle that gutters,
> Mourned by Elector Dust of Brandenburg.
> Dust becomes filth. Whose paws are covered?

Everyone's, finally, as they greet each other

A downfall. But how is it described?
As sacrifice. Today not yet as deed.
So it is: the rule of law that could save lives,

Remains both here and there, by the wayside.
'I spoke as the state,' said a state prosecutor.
'twas recently a comrade Freisler. The Horror.

On the Elector in Kleist's play *The Prince of Homburg*:

The father of this state, the father of all
Does his part, and the others theirs, each his own.
And when there's trouble, there's guilt and penance:
The limits of trust, of the great consensus.

Father Duke does not privilege the troublemaker
As expected, he sees him as one among many
There's not one rule for the wolves, one for the sheep.
But blind tears make help nonsense.

Help for whom? For the next dead men,
Not for the dodger, the one who hides away.
The hero is lured away that he might live.

He may not! And your inner trembling
recedes. But the other guilty man does not
forgive his guilt, though his humanity would require it.

Figure description:
Franz Woyzeck, foot soldier in *Woyzeck* by Georg Büchner
Woyzeck – not a jealousy drama
A man is beaten down due to his dreadful position in an unjust society. When his wife is taken from him he also loses his last hold on a pitiful, small, yet pure self-determination and dignity. The inevitability of the man's destruction becomes clear and unbearable, therefore he takes this self-destruction into his own hands. He kills his wife and gives up on himself. He grabs at the last atom

of self-consciousness (or possibly only self-worth), he saves the last atom of individual humanity he is able to. He gives up on himself and commits a deed that only he can commit, one that destroys him, he who is one with his wife. He becomes a murderer. Woyzeck is the poorest, most exploited, most denigrated man, the one whom progress would benefit most of all, who should able to organise, but for whom there is not yet a party, because he is more exploited and pitiful than his time and society are progressive. Woyzeck – no Jesus Because he has to nail himself to the cross, because the social reality is more terrible than the law that will take him prisoner (the sum is larger than its individual parts).

Definition of a figure:
Baal, poet, in *Baal* by Bertolt Brecht
Baal describes the dialectic of an absolutely purposeful and extreme concern with the self, as evidenced in an individual's stance towards the world: it entails either an extreme and purposeful punishment, indeed destruction, of the individual at the hands the majority, or else (not portrayed in the play) the extreme and purposeful self-realisation of the individual, whether with or without an impact on the majority.

In conclusion I will quote my answer to the publisher Reclam's (Leipzig) 1985 survey 'What would we ask Brecht today?':

To me, every figure or character is the defence of a standpoint or a hope. Every figure has a 'superstructure' story and a personal intellectual history, which are called on by the real story (the sequence of situations and incidents) to account for themselves. A particular figure's problematic, his or her most important element is revealed in the course of the play to be a social construction, and is dissected into power, powerlessness, and utopia. Both stories, when taken seriously, belong together like Siamese twins. Their connection results in a third story: the dialectic one, the real one. In this third story the present can become visible and historically relevant. To formulate it in another way: the opinions represented by a figure lead to a stance, this stance leads, through confrontation with the stances of other figures, to a different opinion and so on. Confrontation is the reality assumed in the theatre.

I've been influenced by people in Russian theatre like the great Stanislavsky and his various pupils whose writings I read. They are, among others: Meyerhold, Tairov, Vakhtangov, Gorchakov. I've also been influenced by comic actors like Chaplin, Keaton and Valentin as well as others whom I will mention later.

I saw a production of Tolstoy's *Anna Karenina* by Vladimir Nemirovich-Danshenko and Vassili Grigoryevich Sachnovski at the Moscow Academic Art Theatre (which was founded by Nemirovich-Danshenko and Konstantin Sergeyevich Stanislavsky). The production of *Anna Karenina* had been running for almost two decades. I was not able to experience the great Alla Konstantinovna Tarassova, because she had shortly before turned her role over to a colleague of hers, whom I found to be most convincing, but whose name I unfortunately don't remember.

The acting was quaint, full of feeling, precise and convincing. There was one scene from the production that left a lasting impression on me: while Anna Karenina is speaking her desperate farewell, a spotlight draws her out of the darkened stage, a darkness which could be a nocturnal landscape or hell. Except for her voice, there is total silence, accentuated through pauses. During one such quiet caesura, two small, barely perceptible points of light appear at a great distance. You think you can hear the pulsating sound of an approaching locomotive. As Anna Karenina's desperation grows, the approaching train, lights fixed on the audience, drives the audience's sympathy to a nightmarish climax: screams mingle with train noises and the locomotive rushes directly into the audience, over the woman who has thrown herself in its path. This scene surely caused cathartic fear. Impressive.

One of the problems presented by empathy really has to do with its straightforward disposition. It prioritises emotions and seeks to reach a truthful performance by deepening (or completing) these emotions. But it becomes apparent that the attempt at this absolute deepening limits the actor's possibilities. He is no longer able criticise the figure he is playing, regardless of the plot of the play. He becomes resistant to the idea of discrediting a figure's actions in a context larger than the play. Put simply, he loses the ability to discriminate or make claims on his figure in the way I believe to be correct. Because just as in real life, where history passes final judgement both subjectively and objectively, it is the plot, the equivalent of history in drama, that makes decisions with and for the performance.

Stanislavsky was of a different opinion. He thought, in accordance with his ideology, that it was character that should primarily hold sway over the figures, that quality of character is somehow immanently present alongside the objective circumstances – not like in Brechtian theatre, where character also has a role to play, but en passant and not as the decisive factor. The truth (or what we assume to be the truth) lies in condemning the social action which the individual is a part of, in the objective facts that can only be registered in hindsight, despite whatever injustices and cruelties become obvious, come to the fore, and nevertheless must be given secondary status in art. Imagination unfolds beyond the figure, if the figure makes it a priority, but remains, nonetheless, within the play. You can also awaken imagination within a figure forcibly, if you see it simply as a part of the dramatic action.

In Nikolai Michailovich Gorchakov's work *Lessons with Stanislavsky*, in the chapter 'Negative Characters', concerning the production of *Armoured Train 14–69*, he records the following conversation between the actors and Stanislavsky:

VISHNEVSKI   I won't shoot at anyone. My Semyon Semyonovich . . .
STANISLAVSKY   No, you'll shoot all right. Like a coward, from the window of your big office! Up there in a crate next to the seismographs are some hand grenades. First you'll throw the crate on to the heads of the workers who are storming your office, then

you'll run as fast as you can out of the rear exit, dress yourself like a worker and tie on one of your servant's aprons. That's how you'll fool the crowd in the street that's tending to the wounded.

VISHNEVSKI   I'm not sure, I'm not totally convinced that I would do that . . .

STANISLAVSKY   Two or three more dinners with General Spassky and you'll do it!

KNIPPER-CHEKHOVA   What? I reckon to play this scene well, I'll have to kill someone too?!

STANISLAVSKY   I've intentionally laid it on a little thick because I see that all the actors in this scene are trying to please the spectator at any cost. I don't find fault with the fact that you want to defend the politics or humanity of your characters – far from it. The problem here has to do with a theatrical sentiment: the lack of courage to stand before the audience as a so-called 'negative' character. You have to get over this.

VISHNEVSKI   But you always say 'seize on the goodness of an evil character'.

STANISLAVSKY   And where are you evil in this scene? [N. Gorchakov, *Regie. Unterricht bei Stanislawski*, Henschel]

For the actor, there is no such thing as a negative figure. An actor's most important task is to defend his figure, so that his figure may be correctly judged, and possibly condemned by the audience. This judgement takes place only on the basis of actual happenings that may, but do not necessarily, correspond to the figure's intentions and opinions. People are judged by world history, not by victims' hatred.

KNIPPER-CHEKHOVA   No, I can't do it. Take whatever you want from me, but I won't kill anyone.

STANISLAVSKY   You needn't kill anyone with your own hands. The soldiers who have been betrayed by General Spassky will kill your enemies for you.

KNIPPER-CHEKHOVA   I won't kill anyone through the hands of others either.

Stanislavsky: That means you're an actress at the Art Theatre and not a landowner from the nobility, not a refugee, not a wicked, harmful mademoiselle.

KNIPPER-CHEKHOVA   Please! I agree with everything you've said – with the landowner, the nobility, the refugee. But why add 'wicked' AND 'harmful' and make me out to almost be a murderer? . . .

STANISLAVSKY   Enemies of progress almost always have negative character traits . . . it's just as honourable to kill the enemy of the state, the fatherland and society with the weapons of art as it is to use those same talents to embody a positive hero of our times . . . killing the enemy means showing the audience this person's inner nature, the source and drive of the person's antisocial behaviour, his or her corrupted psychology . . . that's how deep you have to go into the character of your enemy if you want a performance that is true-to-life. [Ibid.]

First and foremost, it is not a criminal's character traits that distinguish him from others, rather the proof of his unacceptable actions, the list of the atrocities he is responsible for. The fact of having to resort to the character traits of a figure in order to be able to kill innocents or anyone else on stage, even when everything in the actor resists the idea, reveals the helplessness of the emphatic approach. In realistic theatre, no actor can take it upon himself to play a hero or a villain. Realistic theatre rejects the representation of monsters, although humans (who are, after all, the actor's concern) are capable of an astonishing amount of cruelty.

Stanislavsky, who claimed that the terminology he uses is not a product of his own invention but has rather been adapted from 'the practice of students and aspiring actors', who 'lay out their creative feelings in verbal descriptions' while at work, is nevertheless the father of what we have come to know as the 'system'. I find that he's being too modest when he asks for understanding in *An Actor Prepares*:

3

Do not attempt to find a scientific root in these [verbal descriptions]. We have our own dramatic lexicon, our own actor's jargon which has been worked out in real life. To be certain, we also use scientific terms like 'subconscious' or 'intuition'. But we don't use these words in a philosophical sense, rather in an everyday one. It's not our fault that the field of scenic creation has been totally neglected by scholarly inquiry, that it remains unresearched, that we haven't been given the proper vocabulary for practical work. We have to overcome this through our own home-made means, so to speak. [Konstantin Stanislavsky, *Das Geheimnis des schauspielerichen Erfolges*]

This is too deep an obeisance before the scholars, most of whom are just like anyone else, as you can readily discover in their writings on dramaturgy and critical notes on productions.

In the fifties, an essay by Boris Sachawa, a student of Stanislavsky, was recommended to us for study. I only have a typewritten copy of the piece, which is called 'An actor prepares for a role'. I divided the essay into fifty-five points, each of which I responded to.

41

SACHAWA   When an actor steps onto the stage, the audience can already tell if his figure has a life story, even before he has spoken a word. If you can detect the presence of a life story, then you have a fully-formed figure in front of you.

SCHALL   The actor should not allow himself to be concerned with his figure outside the world of the play, even if he feels pressure to do so because he himself knows more than his figure about the background and the outcome of the play (which are expressed through more than just the one figure).

43

SACHAWA   It is just as important that the actor imagine his figure's current lifestyle as it is for him to present a full life story.

SCHALL   The figure's 'current lifestyle' is worthless and superfluous if it does not appear within the plot of the play or is not needed in order to narrate the sequence of events in the play.

44

SACHAWA   The conditions of the figure's current lifestyle need only be hinted at or even not shown at all during the play. The actor, however, should be acquainted with them in great detail. The actor must imagine and experience in great detail his figure's family, living situation, the material conditions of his life and every other circumstance (friends, acquaintances, professional and general milieu). This includes the shape of his wife's nose, even if she does not appear in the play, or even the colour of the wallpaper in his bedroom.

SCHALL   The actual relationships between the figures and their social milieu (and beyond) must be continuously and precisely formulated. The imagination employed for this purpose can be limitless. We should treat the plot of the play, this continuous limitation of the human penchant for exhibitionism, with great care. Things like 'the shape of his wife's nose' and other inconsequential facts can be dispensed with. The realism of a play's own time, combined with the most progressive contemporary thought of the present time, now the realism of socialism, should be the political ally of the content of a work of art, should liberate the content of every style and form.

91 (from an earlier draft that contained ninety-two points)

SACHAWA   Provided that the actor . . ., through practice, has attained an organic mastery of least a few of his figure's physical characteristics, ETUDES AT HOME can be of great use. What do these etudes consist of? An example: in the evening, before going to bed, the actor decides: tomorrow, before I go to the rehearsal, I will perform all my actions as if I were my figure and not myself. When the actor awakens the next morning, he goes about his routine – getting up, washing, dressing, shaving, combing his hair and having breakfast – not in the manner that he is used to, rather as the appropriate figure (Famussov, the Mayor, Tusenbach, Nesmanov, Othello, etc.) would do it.

SCHALL   The epitome of nonsense. What am I supposed to do if I'm playing Ui/Hitler, and I sit at the breakfast table with my non-Aryan family? What am I supposed to do if I want to shave, but have to act like Karl Marx?

Lee Strasberg, head of Stanislavsky's branch in New York, the Actors' Studio, visited Barbara and me in Berlin along with his wife Paula and daughter Susan. They came around the time of our wedding. Paula gave Barbara a gold necklace and Lee, inspired by our conversations, gave me a book (in French) by Boris Sachawa, my rival in the other camp, about Evgeny Bagrationovich Vakhtangov. When I held a seminar in the Actors' Studio later, both of them were deceased. The new head was Elia Kazan. Empathy that has transformation as its goal has always been suspect to me, because I much prefer transformation that might cause empathy. There's a cartoon about the Actors' Studio, the headquarters of the 'System' in the USA, with students like Marilyn Monroe and Marlon Brando: a student, who has empathised himself into a tree, is peed on by a dog who has taken him to be one: success, success! On the other hand the following joke evinces a great respect for Lon Chaney, 'the man with a thousand faces' (who, for example, had all his teeth pulled in order to alter the appearance of his jaw and teeth at will): Chaplin and Keaton are taking a stroll. A worm crawls across their path and Keaton wants to step on it. 'Don't do it', says Chaplin, 'it could be Lon Chaney.'

The various means that actors use to change their appearance have always fascinated me. In *On the Waterfront*, Marlon Brando got injections above his eyebrows in order to simulate the bruises on a boxer's face and in *The Godfather* he stuffed cotton into the pouches of his cheeks, which made his jaw more difficult to move and gave it a grinding quality. In *The Playboy of the Western World* Harry Gillmann had enormous bowlegs sewn into his trousers to play Old Mahon. For *Señora Carrar's Rifles*, Weigel had a corset made that was hard as bone, in order to continuously emphasise the inflexibility of her intention not to send her sons to war. When I played Kalle in *Conversations in Exile*, I had myself fitted with lead cuffs to make it harder to move my arms. Through these modifications, unnecessary concentration is reduced, leaving the actor free to concentrate on the real matter at hand. But these means remain mere reinforcement, and do not replace the confidence that you must have in assuming stances and producing gestures to change your appearance – it doesn't have to be a complete mutation. In *Arturo Ui*, Brecht has Inna say to Roma:

It's a funny thing about tobacco. When a man
Is smoking, he looks calm. And if you imitate
A calm-looking man and light a cigarette, you
Get to be calm yourself.

In spite of his antipathy towards them, Brecht was not strictly against pure feelings. When Angelika Hurwicz as Grusha gave her love free rein for the helpless child during one scene in *The Caucasian Chalk Circle*, he told her something like: Go ahead, do it. Love, but make sure that your reason returns at the right time. I had the same goal when I gave a speech as Ui: to win the audience over through empathy and deep, earnest, almost private ingratiation, only to shove them away again, once I felt that the seduction was complete.

As far as Antonin Artaud's theatre is concerned, it's rather foreign to me, not because it rubs me the wrong way or I don't like it, but because I've never experienced a convincing performance. However, his prose pieces are delicacies which, in their destructive imprecision and limitless claims, seem to be universally valid and overpowering. They recall *Les Chants de Maldoror* ('Maldoror': 'gilder of evil' or 'dawn of evil') by Isidore Lucien Ducasse, who published them under the pseudonym Comte de Lautréamont. Heiner Müller was especially fond of them. In Artaud's essays and texts collected in *The Theater and its Double*, the pronouncements pile up:

No More Masterpieces . . .

Past masterpieces are fit for the past: they are no good to us. We have the right to say what has been said and even what has not been said in a way that belongs to us, responding in a direct and straight-forward manner to present-day feelings everybody can understand.

Theatre and Cruelty . . .

In the anguished, catastrophic times we live in, we feel an urgent need for theatre that is not overshadowed by events, but arouses deep echoes within us and predominates over our unsettled period . . .

Everything that acts is cruelty. Theatre must rebuild itself on a concept of this drastic action pushed to the limit . . .

Moreover, to speak clearly, the imagery in some paintings by Grünewald or Hieronymus Bosch gives us a good enough idea of what a show can be, where things outside nature appear as temptations just as they would in a saint's mind.

Theatre must rediscover its true meaning in this spectacle of a temptation, where life stands to lose everything and the mind to gain everything.

The Theatre of Cruelty (First Manifesto)

We cannot go on prostituting the idea of a theatre whose only value lies in its agonising, magical relationship to reality and danger . . .

From the foregoing it becomes apparent that theatre will never recover its own specific powers of action until it has recovered its own language. That is, instead of harking back to texts regarded as sacred and definitive, we must first break theatre's subjugation to the text, and rediscover the idea of a kind of unique language somewhere in between gesture and thought. [Artaud, *Collected Works 4*, trans. Victor Corti]

In the section of his book titled 'The Programme', which describes the repertoire of his later theatre, he makes clear from the beginning: 'We shall stage, without regard for text.'

Nine intentions follow, including:

8. Büchner's *Woyzeck*, in a spirit of reaction against our own principles and as an example of what can be drawn from a formal text in terms of the stage.
9. Works of the Elizabethan theatre, stripped of their texts and retaining only the former accoutrements of period, situations, characters and action. [Ibid.]

In supplemental documents appended to Artaud's book *The Theatre and Its Double*, the umbilical cord to the past and tradition is cut explicitly:

The Theatre and the Plague . . .

Theatre is not an art.

Art in a dispassionate sense, in the sense of copying life, is a Western idea. It may well be a rule here on earth that the conditioning of matter ought to lie in this imitative inability, but no artistic production is of any value without the feeling of this inability, and the active, aggravated consciousness of what, just by being alive, has consequently been lost. All mental activity is useless without constant reference to powers, without efforts which waste one away but exercise a critical faculty. True mental exercise sucks life as dry as a disease. [Ibid.]

Jerzy Grotowski, a director, theatre manager and teacher of an acting technique, claimed in 1967:

We are entering the age of Artaud. The 'Theatre of Cruelty' has been canonised, i.e., made trivial, swapped for trinkets, tortured in various ways. When an eminent creator with an achieved style and personality, like Peter Brook, turns to Artaud, it's not to hide his own weaknesses, or to ape the man. It just happens that at a given point of his development he finds himself in agreement with Artaud, feels the need of confrontation, 'tests' Artaud and retains whatever stands up to this test. [Grotowski, *Towards a Poor Theatre*]

More than any other, Grotowski comes closest to Artaud's ideal of theatre.

In a lecture, Peter Brook says:

> The Holy Theatre . . .
> [Grotowski's theatre] is a complete way of life for all its members, and so it is in contrast with most other avant-garde and experimental groups whose work is scrambled and usually invalidated through lack of means . . .
>
> Grotowski makes poverty an ideal; his actors have given up on everything except their own bodies; they have the human instrument and limitless time – no wonder they feel the richest theatre in the world. [Peter Brook, *The Empty Space*]

I've seen one of Grotowski's productions and two of Brook's. If I accept Grotowski's opinion that 'the paradox of Artaud lies in the fact that it is impossible to carry out his proposals', I can still allow myself to be concerned with him and accept a certain amount of his influence.

My memory of the production of Wyspianski's *Akropolis* at Grotowski's Laboratory Theatre in Lodz is hazy. It was during the Berliner Ensemble's 1952 tour. We few spectators who were there sat among the props, grey relicts of extermination camps, each person in a different place. The action unfolded around us without drawing us in; we remained observers. In this small room, Auschwitz was conveyed to us by prisoners and SS men. What remains in my memory, however, is how I left the performance shaking my head, unaffected although a German, because I had had the impression, even without understanding the language, that I had been supposed to see only undifferentiated victims, all equally pitiable, all sticking fast in the blood and muck of history. When Weigel brought me with her once to a meeting with Grotowski, we sat across from each other, respectfully and tactfully, but completely unable to create or feel understanding for each other. Unfortunately, I have never seen Grotowski's world-famous production of Calderón's *The Constant Prince*.

One performance of *Woyzeck* that I saw in Turin (the name of the director escapes me), which was supposedly indebted to the Theatre of Cruelty, proved to be a physically gruelling tour de force for the actors. A sort of canted wall, made of good, light, polished wood like climbing walls in a school gymnasium, stretched from deep at the back of the small stage diagonally across the stage from left to right (or right to left). The impossibility or unspeakable difficulty of overcoming this wall without the risk of injury or death determined the space within which the scenes could move, where they were carried out like athletic contests. The actual cruelty which, in the play, grows like a sweet poisonous flower from the soil of the couple's affectionate misery, did not come across in performance. This was prevented by the brutality, which was continuously performed in all its abnormality. The fierce desperation brought on by love, which is constant from scene to scene and is the way that Woyzeck can approach his wife, this desperation that becomes a wild rage in the end, was not taken into consideration during the performance.

I saw Peter Brook's production of *A Midsummer Night's Dream* in all its perfection, although this perfection came with a caveat. During a public discussion in London between him and some members of the Berliner Ensemble, Brook had made us aware of the neglect of the mother–son relationship in our production of *Coriolanus*. His criticism corresponded to our own misgivings (mine especially, because I played Coriolanus), and so we started rehearsals after the tour and changed this relationship. Volumnia's entreaty to her arrogant son became Rome's actual victory over the traitor. For this change, we now preferred not only political means, but also interpersonal means, which opened up Shakespeare's work more than our previous interpretation, which had been too deterministic. Through Brook, we were made aware that:

> The scene between Coriolanus and his mother pretty much makes up the core of the entire play: like the storm in *Lear*, or a monologue in *Hamlet*, the emotional content of this scene provides

the heat that welds the strictness of cool-headed thinking to the structure of dialectic confrontation. Without the clash of the two protagonists in its most intense form, the story remains impotent. When we leave the theatre, we're less pestered by the memory. The strength of the scene between Coriolanus and his mother consists exactly of those elements that do not necessarily make clear sense. [Brook, ibid.]

The subtitle and the first few sentences of Brook's book *The Empty Space* refer to the return of theatre to its authentic being.

I can take any empty space and call it a bare stage. A man walks across this empty space whilst someone else is watching him, and this is all that is needed for an act of theatre to be engaged. [Ibid.]

He consistently promotes the closed nature of theatre. In his production of *A Midsummer Night's Dream* he went a step further than anyone I've known before him and did not allow the branch-and-root complex of the play to be determined by natural forms, thus accepting impulses which would normally not be allowed the story because they do not originate from within it. From supports and scaffolding, the actors who were not immediately involved in the scene playfully accompanied and interfered with the action, using nets, poles, belts and other improvised props to create obstacles, entanglements, twists, turns and opportunities for confusion. This would usually have been done through an imitation of nature, especially when, as in this case, most of the scenes take place in the forest. Some time before the Brook Ensemble's guest performance, the Deutsche Theater in Berlin premiered Peter Hack's *Die Sorgen und die Macht*. I remembered the performance of an embittered old Nazi, who complained about the new circumstances and conditions in East Germany, mumbling grimly into his beard: 'If I only had just a little Hitler!' He underscored the modesty of his wish by forming a small space between his thumb and forefinger. When I left the theatre after the performance of *A Midsummer Night's Dream* I mumbled, 'If I only had just a little tree!'

But the representation of even the tiniest fir tree had been denied me. Brook wanted to destroy any point of reference to nature and create it anew. The acting was excellent, if not astonishing. He described his approach in this way:

> It is a strange role, that of the director: he does not ask to be God and yet his role implies it. He wants to be fallible, and yet an instinctive conspiracy of the actors is to make him the arbiter, because an arbiter is so desperately wanted all the time. In a sense the director is always an imposter, a guide at night who does not know the territory, and yet he has no choice – he must guide, learning the route as he goes. Deadliness often lies in wait when he does not recognise this situation, and hopes for the best, when it is the worst that he needs to face. [Ibid.]

Brook is an exceptional director. It's touching to read that he is not very much different from the majority of directors when it comes to the arrogance of his profession.

The Living Theatre, Judith and Julian Beck and their troupe, impressed me the most in regard to Artaud. They performed *The Brig* by Kenneth Brown, a dramatised documentation of oppression, humiliation and the destruction of human will [*Menschenzerbrechen*] in a US military prison. It was a dark stage full of outrage, whose sequences of arithmetic rows were without end. I remember the ferocity of the collective movement, the suffering portrayed and the shouted orders: rhythmically ear splitting, painful and pitiless. Their method of acting was ecstatically precise and breathtaking but swept the spectators along in hatred for the power of their own country.

According to Imke Buchholz and Judith Malina in their book about the Living Theatre,

> During this period the influence of Artaud's Theatre of Cruelty is clearly recognisable – a period of the denunciation of human suffering. Theatre must restore culture to life, must tear down walls and expand consciousness. [Buchholz and Malina, *Living (heißt leben) Theater*, Trikont]

One consequence of this explosive performance is that it

> puts the Living Theatre in the sights of the Internal Revenue Service. The theatre is closed and legal proceedings against Julian and Judith begin. Julian tells the press that he intends to keep performing after the closure of the theatre, on city streets and squares . . . After being invited to London, the Living Theatre leaves America and enters voluntary European exile. When the legal proceedings are taken up again, Julian and Judith return, act as their own defence and are sentenced to sixty and thirty days in jail respectively. [Ibid.]

I met with this important man of the theatre, this zealot (who was actually very gentle), for the last time in New York in 1985, where he was already marked by death.

> We [the Living Theatre] have made it our goal to restore theatre's function as a medium of transcendence and liberation from the kiss of the whip. [Ibid.]

Contrary to Artaud, in life and in drama, even the most hardy person is not determined solely as an individual (with the same stamp and brand as other individuals) but through the relationships among and between a number of other people. Artaud, who must have been very lonely himself, didn't recognise this as a driving force or didn't think it worth experiencing.

For me, Samuel Beckett is, like Brecht, one of the greatest writers of the century. He wrote that

> the theatre is not a moral institution in Schiller's sense. I want neither to indoctrinate nor improve nor distract the people from their boredom. I want to bring poetry into drama, a kind of poetry that has travelled through nothingness and finds a new beginning in a new space. I think in new dimensions and it really doesn't matter much to me who can follow along. [Beckett in *Spectaculum VI. Sieben Moderne Theaterstücke*]

He has often been counted among the writers of the Theatre of the Absurd, but I've always been of the opinion that his work dispenses with the absurd, with exaggeration, even the late plays, which seem like strange etudes. Through him, reality, in being imitated, gained a slowness, which he emphasised until the slowness came to a halt. But in this decisive stillness movement remained, even when it was no longer possible. Stillness is not death, just the inability to change oneself, to move oneself forward or in any other capacity.

I played Krapp in *Krapp's Last Tape*. During an interview with the journalist Dieter Kranz I advanced the opinion that:

> Krapp is a lively figure, who, admittedly, has reached an end point. When he approaches his past in listening to the tape, he discovers that he made decisions at certain points in his life that nudged his further development in the wrong direction. First he attempts to put his mistakes behind him: I am what I am. But this doesn't succeed. He rewinds the tape once again to the description of the only meaningful human relationship he has ever had. As he listens to it again, he freezes, and (at least this is how I play it) it breaks his heart. This is a powerful scene. Not even every important Shakespeare role reaches such a desperate greatness at the end. David Gothard, the English theatre man, remarked how Beckett said at rehearsals that the role must be played so the audience knows Krapp will die this very night. He will not continue to exist as a fossil, will not persist as a living corpse; he will really die. I try to convey that in my acting.

And from an interview with the journalist Jonathan Kalb:

> Nevertheless, I think that in all his plays, even in *Krapp's Last Tape*, another movement is present, namely a realisation. . . . He looks for the place on the tape with the woman in the boat, the place with her offer and his refusal. At the end he comes to a strong, emotional conclusion (surprising even to him) and suddenly, for the first time, he is no longer able to bear it. There *is* development in the play.

BBS adds:

The saddest part of the whole thing for me is that in such a long life, the highlight was a short love affair many years ago. And he feeds on it practically his entire life. You get the feeling that this one tape comes up again and again, it was the high point of his life, and yet so insignificant.

On 28 January 1986, Barbara wrote to 38 Boulevard Saint Jacques, 75014 Paris:

Dear Mr Beckett,

My husband Ekkehard Schall and I are genuinely pleased to be finally working on your play *Krapp's Last Tape*. I believe we have a friend in common – David Gothard – and with his encouragement I would like to ask you if it would be possible, or if you would be interested in leading rehearsals for your play in Berlin for the final two weeks or ten days. We anticipate that it will be performed on 14 July of this year in the Theater im Palast (TiP). It would be a great joy and honour for us. With fond greetings and wishes for a good 1986,

Yours,

Barbara Brecht-Schall

The answer came immediately in sharp, angular handwriting:

Dear Mrs Brecht-Schall,
Thank you for your letter from 6 February,
and for your friendly invitation,
which I am unfortunately unable to accept.
My travelling days are over.
With renewed good wishes
for your performance of Krapp,
I remain cordially yours,
Samuel Beckett

Beckett's poetry and his love for the poetry of others spilled over into each other.

... Scalded the eyes out of me reading *Effie* again, a page a day, with tears again. *Effie* . . . [*Pause.*] Could have been happy with her, up there on the Baltic, and the pines, and the dunes. [*Pause.*] Could I? [*Pause.*] And she? [*Pause.*] Pah! [*Pause.*] Fanny came in a couple of times. Bony old ghost of a whore. Couldn't do much, but I suppose better than a kick in the crutch. The last time wasn't so bad. How do you manage it, she said, at your age? I told her I'd been saving up for her all my life. [*Pause.*] Went to vespers once, like when I was in short trousers. [*Pause. Sings.*]

Now the day is over,
Night is drawing nigh-igh,
Shadows – (*coughing, then almost inaudible*) –
of the evening
Steal across the sky.
[Beckett, *The Complete Dramatic Works*]

Beckett's plays will become larger than life only when the frozen wastes and ossification have fatally affected every individual's and family's ability to live. Many of Brecht's plays will also have to wait until social conditions, which are miserable, brutally push the underclass on top again and expose the countless ways it has been victimised and mutilated.

Brecht wrote about Chinese theatre twice in his *Writings on Theatre* collected in the Suhrkamp edition, but it seems to me that he never saw any Chinese theatre besides the female impersonator Dr Mei Lan-Fang's May 1935 performance in Moscow, which he quite admired. At least he doesn't describe any other performances. And his interest was clear: he was looking for support for and examples of the type of theatre he envisioned. For him 'Alienation effects in Chinese Acting' and 'Doubled Showing' were just the thing. He must have been happy to be able to report in 'On the Art of Being a Spectator':

At first glance it seems that this art (which negotiates so many contracts with the spectator, makes so many rules about how the spectator is to relate to it), an art that is not immediately understandable, not only in emotional terms, is meant for a small circle of scholars or initiates. One discovers however that this is in no way the case: this theatre is understood by the common people as well. [Brecht, GW 15]

His dream audience really existed – it was Chinese. And the Chinese actors were the kind that he wished for.

He expresses his awareness of being watched. . . . the artist observes himself. Thus if he is representing a cloud, perhaps, showing its unexpected appearance, its soft and strong growth, its rapid yet gradual transformation, he will occasionally look at the audience as if to say: isn't it just like that? At the same time he also observes his own arms and legs, adducing them, testing them and perhaps finally approving them. . . . In this way the artist separates mime (showing observation) from gesture (showing a cloud), but without detracting from the latter, since the body's attitude is reflected in the face and is wholly responsible for its expression. At one moment the expression is of well-managed restraint; at another of utter triumph. The artist has been using his countenance as a blank sheet, to be inscribed by the *Gestus* of the body.

Brecht had found his actor. Such an actor could be produced, or educated, but only within a generations-long tradition in an ancient culture that had endured in a people. It reminded me of the story about the English lawn. A guest is admiring the lawn in front of a manor and asks: 'How do you get it to look like that?' The answer: 'It's very simple. You have to cut and water it daily.' Question: 'For how long?' Answer: 'A few centuries.'

One thing that I agree with is:

The artist's object is to appear strange and even surprising to the audience. He achieves this by looking strangely at himself and his work. As a result everything put forward by him has a touch of the amazing. Everyday things are thereby raised above the level of the obvious and automatic.

This is a constant reminder for me: 'The performer plays incidents of utmost passion, but without his delivery becoming heated.' The female impersonator who made such an impression on Brecht did not imitate women as a man, but rather described them, as an actor, which is something very different.

[Mei Lan-Fang] demonstrates certain feminine movements while wearing a dinner jacket. There are two distinct figures: one does the showing, the other is being shown. In the evening, one of them (the doctor, family man and banker) shows even more of the other: her face, her clothes, the way she looks when she is astonished, jealous or cheeky, her voice. The figure in the dinner jacket has almost disappeared completely. . . . But he emphasises that his greatest accomplishment is not that he can walk and cry like a woman, but rather like a particular woman. His opinions about what is 'essential' to this woman are his main concern: something critical, philosophical about the woman. [Brecht GW 15]

As you can gather from the text, Brecht saw Mei Lan-Fang perform twice in a single day. He was, you could say, a fan. In his journal he mentions a Chinese author and actor named Tsiang, who didn't impress him very much, but whom he found to be 'extremely interesting':

9 july 43

then he comes out here and demonstrates a few points to helli and me. he shows how the chinese, using a stick as a gun, simply take the stick as a symbol for the gun; he treats the stick as a gun, stresses how heavy it is, brings out the roundness of the butt etc. up to this point it is the technique of illusion à la stanislavsky, but then he agrees with me that the real art begins when the gun itself is treated as a stick being treated as a gun, i.e. when the gun itself is distanced. so it is not a matter of the gun's appearing to be no more (if no less) than a gun, but of the gun's having something said about it (recounted, raised for discussion, exposed to associations if you like). [Translation modified]

Accuracy was important to Brecht, though not always. At the Berliner Ensemble in 1954, as we practised the Chinese popular drama by Lo Ding, Tschang Fan and Tschu Dschin-Nan translated into German as *Hirse für die Achte* (friendship still ruled between China and the Soviet Union) our Chinese advisers, including the translator Yuan Miau-Tse, told us the following after they saw our provisional stage design: 'We don't sit on such low stools in front of such low tables that are almost on the floor. In almost every household the chairs and tables have legs as long as yours here.' It was rather embarrassing to us and the director Manfred Wekwerth because it looked so nice and foreign, like, well, a not-so-modern culture. What to do? Ask Brecht. The case was brought before him and his decision was: the stools stay, otherwise people will accuse us of not having done our research. That was a canny reading of popular taste and not just of the Germans': later someone showed us photos of a Peking performance of Schiller's *Love and Intrigue* in which all the actors were blond and Luise and Sophie had long, thick braids.

In the Berliner Ensemble's performance I played the local commander, an officer in the Japanese occupying force in China, and was surrounded by exceptional actors like Raimund Schelcher, Fred Düren, Heinz Schubert, Friedrich Gnaß, Norbert Christian, Peter Kalisch and others, all of whom played the good and clever Chinese. I exaggerated my figure to the point of recognisability: I wanted to show an uptight, crippled villain at first glance. I stood and walked in the first position *plié* (back then I did classical exercise at the bar every day), my upper arm pressed sideways against my ribcage, gesticulating wildly with my lower arm only, my voice on a single tone, high and sharp as a knife. I was the only one who was not speaking German, but rather what was probably Japanese with lots of drawn-out Aaahs, Ooohs and Eees. My military hat had a long, even visor, which sat directly on my eyebrows, and when I approached Raimund Schelcher, who played the mayor, I pushed myself against him threateningly, shoved the visor deep between my teeth and gazed menacingly into his eyes, which were above the visor. It was a wonderful attempt to eliminate every trace of naturalness, and therefore in the least suitable way to denounce a figure who really would have earned denunciation. I used this figure without scruple for the purpose of trying out as many techniques and methods as possible.

Then the day came when Brecht was to come to rehearsal. Everyone was scared for me, myself included, so Wekwerth said to me: 'Make him laugh. He'll never forbid something that he's laughed at.' And so I tried it. I walked over the above-mentioned stools with my knees bent to the same level as their seats, my nose and shoulders walking on in a straight line as if they had noticed nothing of the action down below (I'd seen Chaplin do that), I played the hell out of it, until, thank God, I heard Brecht's laughter, or the bleating that was his laughter. Afterwards Brecht said something to me like 'I don't approve of what you're doing. But I think you need it, so go ahead and play it like that. In two years, you yourself won't want to play it that way.' He was right. Two years later Lothar Bellag took over the role. I couldn't play it the same way any more.

Once, in Berlin, I saw the Peking Opera perform a piece with song, dance and a large cast, called *The White-Haired Girl* (there's also a film with the same title). It was a mixture of operetta and martial arts, at once patriotic and sentimental. To me even the decor was kitschy. In contrast, Kabuki theatre made a powerful impression on me.

> The name [Kabuki] means a fashionable warrior costume: a long, broad garment, a headscarf that covers the lower part of the face, and two swords tucked into the belt,

writes Josef Gregor in his *Weltgeschichte des Theaters* [World History of the Theatre]. I'm of the opinion that I saw such a production in the theatre, but I couldn't swear to it. Maybe it was just a television broadcast. In any case I have a lively visual memory of it. Naturally, ceremony stood in the foreground: opulent costumes (which required special movements and gaits), strict performance (which transformed the stage into a distant isle without any trace of romance) and masculine strength (which melded itself to the representation of a woman) combined to create a sense of the ancient, which was for me new and threatening. But one thing left me speechless: the vocal performance, the cranial resonance (we know the resonance zones from the chest and throat up to the frontal sinus, we're able to speak with a powerful chest voice or sing with a delicate head voice). The actor's entire body appeared to be vibrating due to the unbelievable tension required to produce that certain pitch at which articulation is still possible, but which is no longer of this world. His voice seemed to flow from the back of his skull, from where the soft spot on his head used to be, filling the performance space almost visibly. Incredible. I was so delighted that I never forgot it; and I knew, from then on, that I would begin to make theatre in a different way than I had learned.

My most useful experiences with Asian performance came from the films of Akira Kurosawa. I saw *Rashoman* early on. The film tells of a duel between a bandit and a samurai (or maybe just a nobleman), who defends his wife and is killed. His wife is subsequently raped. The film tells many different versions of this story. It was the film's refusal to assign guilt that really astonished me, the way that the atrocity was erased as such through the sequence of various stories and experiences, extinguished like a weak candle, blown on first from one side and then from the other. It was also astonishing how the foreign culture of Kurosawa's *Throne of Blood* transformed Shakespeare's *Macbeth* into a play at once new and ancient.

Seven years after I gave this seminar in Milan, I saw Giorgio Strehler's production of Johann Wolfgang Goethe's *Faust, A Tragedy in Two Parts* at the same place. It was the most opulent visit to the theatre that I have ever had the pleasure of enjoying. In the Scuola di Teatro he had had a theatre built that, with its round main floor, combined the advantages of a circus ring or arena (instead of a pit) with the conventional (but not elevated) proscenium stage. The wooden panels and clearly visible equipment gave the stage a look both majestic and modern. On both evenings, most of the scenes took place in the round inner part of the stage, surrounded by spectators, who sat stacked in narrow tiers from floor to ceiling. A few interior scenes took place in the box-like part of the rear stage. Strehler's technique was triumphant in implementing his vision through magical and fantastic effects. After a long silence, Mephistopheles's minions emerge quietly from a dark, softly gurgling body of water (obviously the entrance to the underworld), ready to follow his orders. Spotlights create a narrow shaft of light that cuts through the darkness from a great height, penetrating Faust's cell-like study and tracing the patterns of his thoughts. In the second part Strehler is enthroned as Pluto upon the back of an elephant that excretes money.

> My dear masters of the theatrical arts Giorgio Strehler and Ekkehard Schall,
> My dear Mrs Brecht,
> Mr Prefect,
> dear guests,

begins a laudatory speech that the General Consulate of the Federal Republic of Germany held in honour of Giorgio and me in Milan,

> today is the beginning of the German week of Giorgio Strehler's European Faust Festival. André Suarès, who was certainly no friend of the Germans, said once of Goethe: 'Europe – c'est un mot vide sans lui.' Europe is an empty word without him. The Germans never really understood this. They made him into the 'Greatest Poet of All Time', which sounds dreadfully close to the 'Greatest Field Marshal of All Time'. They made him into their 'national poet'. Naturally, this wasn't a perfect fit. Goethe himself said once that an eagle doesn't really care if it's flying over Saxony-Anhalt or Saxony-Weimar. This eagle was made the head of a German chicken farm

where the German theatre people and German Goethe professors played the chickens. But they couldn't fly. You, dear Mr Strehler, have made him once again into the eagle that he is. You've let him grow wings again and take to the skies over Europe, which is his homeland and the homeland of all great European artists . . .

Bert Brecht, because he was, among other things, one of the most important theatre directors of this century, could barely stomach productions of his own plays put on by others. He took the whole lot of them for misunderstandings. With one exception: Giorgio Strehler. For similar reasons Goethe didn't go to the premiere of his *Faust* in Weimar. But I'm fairly certain: he would have come to your production.

Strehler had a one-of-a-kind personality. He was irresistible in his self-importance; endearing, actually. I saw him and Milva on stage in the Piccolo Teatro, during the premiere of their Brecht Programme. He watched her attentively as she sang, ever the director, correcting her tersely and quickly in front of the audience, right in the middle of her performance. Once I saw him coming towards me during the final applause for our performance of *Life of Galileo* in Milan at the Teatro Lirico. Exhausted, I bowed together with my colleagues and received a great ovation, from Giorgio as well, whose claps and shouts of 'bravo!' slowly penetrated the crowd's acclamation. He stood at the rear of a long hall with a middle aisle stretching to the stage and he started to approach me slowly, all the while clapping and looking to his left and right, spurring his fellow *Milanesi* on to further applause. As he took the first few steps leading to the middle of the stage, the audience saw him, their matador, and continued applauding with reserved apprehension, observing him as he looked on admiringly. He had elevated me in the eyes of the crowd through this action and when he stood beside me, humbly, almost alone on stage, we embraced and the house exploded again in jubilation, a jubilation meant for him more than anyone, for he had found my Galileo wonderful and was not embarrassed to show it.

In the Schiller Theater in Berlin I saw his production of William Shakespeare's *King Lear*. In his 'Notes on *King Lear*' Strehler writes:

In my preliminary notes there is a completely intuitive observation: Fool – Cordelia! When Cordelia disappears, the Fool appears, and when the Fool disappears, Cordelia appears again. That's obvious. But in and of itself, it doesn't justify identification between Cordelia and the Fool. Certainly it causes a sort of 'premonition' like from a strange queasy feeling, from a correspondence that is more obvious when watching the scene than it is when reading. No more than that . . .

One thing appears certain to me, however: there's something mysterious in this link between Cordelia and the Fool, something that's not apparent from the outside. You can't explain this, you have to feel it. Even Bradley spoke of a fool who 'loves Cordelia and stayed back to suffer when Cordelia departed'. He's much more Cordelia's Fool than Lear's. In a certain sense, it seems that the Fool is a kind of 'extension' of Cordelia's presence . . . To me the most mysterious truth is the following: the Fool is the 'persistence' of the good that has been driven away . . . The Fool-Cordelia problem is surely one of the most puzzling, craziest problems that I've ever encountered. It's so strange that you have to ask yourself if it really exists, or if it's just a figment of your imagination. [Giorgio Strehler, '*Notizen zu* Re Lear', *Programmheft*]

This is an extremely interesting constellation, which can be accounted for by the fact that during Elizabethan times the same actor had to play both the Fool and Cordelia. Anything beyond this is a matter of endless speculation. Anyway, in Strehler's production one actress played both roles and I would have liked to have been able to follow her performance, but I couldn't make out anything on stage, because it was dark for four and a half hours. In addition to that the masks and costumes obscured any possible unity or connection between the two figures. For this reason I was completely astonished when, after the performance, Giorgio asked my opinion of this particular phenomenon, which was so near and dear to him. Since I hadn't studied the play programme, I hadn't noticed it. My impression was a

> Dark Performance [*Vorstellung*] (*Lear* by Strehler)
> The 'dark threshold of time' dark time, dark weather, a storm, dark conditions in the human soul, dark feelings, black hatred, insanity overcoming the spirit like the night enveloping nature– showing all this darkness on a darkened stage is like reading Novalis's 'Hymns to the Night' outside on a moonless night in a barely audible tone, like viewing a Rembrandt in the dark, hanging it in a cellar. The brightness of the world is the gauge of darkness, and the burdensome night of a work of art requires brightness (of the day, of the public sphere, of the electric light) in order to be recognisable and assessable, in order to make an impression.

In the pantheon of the performing arts the great comedians fly about. Droves of great silent-film comedians buzz this way and that – praise be to Charlie Chaplin, Buster Keaton, Harry Langdon, Harold Lloyd and Ben Turpin. In contrast, the great tragedians sit on the rocky ground, the visionaries among them on benches in the round, their gazes directed towards the high middle part of the ceiling, where a small opening makes visible a patch of sky. Comical effects, more than tragic ones, are related to contradictions – even if these contradictions are only apparent ones and may be produced mechanically. The most wonderful contradictions, as you know, are the tragicomic ones. They are mainly contradictions of the spirit in life or of life in the spirit. Just as the dissatisfied Faust is driven into the spiritual realm by life, the efforts of study and learning (to the loss of reality, to gambling with his soul), so the spiritual realm drives him back into human life (to love, sexuality, deceit, betrayal, a lust for riches and exploitation), frightened, even into the realm of the mothers. This ageing man's mid-life crisis is comic, the attempt of the young Faust to escape it at the expense of others (at absolutely no cost to himself, if possible) is tragic, and the continual movement from scepticism to faith and back again is tragicomic. Comedy certainly requires an actor to have a talent all his own. Nevertheless it must be learned, although it is seldom taught. Many beginners who see themselves as lovers and heroes are pushed into comedy because of their appearance. Perhaps they are scrawny, have a big schnoz or potbelly, or maybe they waddle, stagger, have two left feet or are otherwise awkward. But [Karl] Valentin's grumpiness and abysmal misreading of other people is due to more than his thin figure, which he exploits to the fullest extent, and [Hans] Moser's obtuseness and confusion are due to more than his mumbling or his poker face. Situational comedy and verbal comedy are clearly distinct, as their names state. It is a happy accident when one supports the other, e.g. when Felix Bressart (in Ernst Lubitsch's film *To Be or Not To Be*), playing a Jewish actor whose deepest, impossible wish is to play Shylock once in his life, begins to speak the part of Shylock in a theatre foyer in occupied Warsaw, while surrounded by SS men. He is under a great deal of stress, but not yet in danger, because he has not yet been recognised as a Jew. Craftily averting his doom, he avoids the premise 'I am a Jew' and every other reference to 'Jew' or 'Christian'. It is simple, naive, sentimental and endlessly tragic.

The Merchant of Venice by William Shakespeare
Act III Scene I
Shy. . . . Hath a Jew not eyes? hath not a Jew hands, organs, dimensions, senses, afflictions, passions? fed with the same food, hurt with the same weapons, subject to the same diseases, heal'd by the same means, warm'd and cool'd by the same winter and summer as a Christian is? If you prick us do we not bleed? If you tickle us, do we not laugh? If you poison us, do we not die? and if you wrong us, shall we not revenge?

In the film the scene sounds like this:

How did you get here?
I was born here.
Whom do you wish to see here?

Him.

And what do you want from our Führer?

What does he want from us? What does he want from Poland?

What does he want? Why? What?

Are we not men? Have we not hands, organs, senses, dimensions, emotions, passions? Fed with the same food, hurt with the same weapons, subject to the same diseases, healed by the same means, warmed and cooled by the same winter and summer? If you prick us, do we not bleed? If you poison us, do we not die? And if you wrong us, shall we not avenge ourselves?

Lieutenants Lang and Schneider, – Jawohl! – take this man back to headquarters, I want to question him.

Situational comedy:

It always tickles your funny bone when a fool's life is in danger and he does not notice it, and the danger passes him by at the last minute without the slightest action on his part. His partner, the would-be perpetrator, helps him by stepping on to the mousetrap just as thunder rolls outside, and is hit by lightning as he tiptoes towards the innocent, slumbering victim with the intention of slitting his throat. In this situation both parties help each other to be funny, whereby one of them (usually the stupid, clueless victim) often profits more than the other. Comedy is created through an incongruity that the spectator is aware of, which leads to some sort of inevitable outcome. The spectator awaits this outcome with pleasure, and when it finally arrives he can exhale in relief. The comedian doesn't understand the obvious and apparent incongruity, or doesn't take notice of it. It can come from many different situations: in the repetition or demonstration of an action that is completely safe, like an empty revolver, which in the decisive moment turns out to be loaded after all and goes off, or even hits someone. Or the incongruity can come, for example, from the claim that a certain house is so secure that there has never been a murder there, just like in Frank Capra's film *Arsenic and Old Lace* where it's an absolute certainty that there is no corpse in the chest next to the window.

When Cary Grant seeks to confirm this claim with a lift of the lid and a quick glance inside, he notices that there really is a corpse in the chest. Or it can come from the logic with which a prisoner sticks exactly to a plan, even though the audience has long since noticed that the tunnel he is digging leads directly into the police station because he is holding the map upside down.

The comedian only has to declare something to be wrong, which is clear to everyone else, only has to develop a plan, which he alone does not see the folly of, and he has laughter on his side (or at his expense, depending on how you see it). The actor gladly uses a sort of over-exuberance, which causes him to push all the train cars on to the wrong track, or a briskness or lively confidence, the kind he needs to kick a much smaller man in the rear, without noticing that the man has gone away and has been replaced by a surly giant. Or he plays the helplessness of an ox in front of a new gate, in a situation that can be overcome through play. Or he shows cheekiness (or to put it better, impudence) in a dangerous situation: like a naked man, who, when discovered in his lover's bedroom closet, bows quickly to her furious husband and asks him when the next bus to Podunk Junction leaves. Or he manages a situation brilliantly but unusually (and in fact unsuitably), like when Charlie Chaplin plays a social worker in a film (the title of which escapes me) who takes a bag of chips into a tenement room so full of children that he scatters the chips all over the ground like feed for chickens. Or the comedian shows an orderliness which will not be stopped by any kind of danger or hazard, such as Buster Keaton exhibits in *The General*, when he calmly heats the loco-motive's tender with tree branches and trunks in order to escape the middle of the battlefield, where troops from the Union and the Confederacy are firing on one another. He inspects each piece of wood expertly, throwing it into the furnace only if it has no knots, otherwise he throws it away. Just like in *The Navigator*, when he stands on the bridge as the captain during the launch, and dips straight into the water and goes under, motionless and proud, hand raised to the brim of his hat in salute.

In John Millington Synge's *The Playboy of the Western World* I played Shawn Keogh, a coward in love with Pegeen Mike (played wonderfully by Barbara). Pegeen stood behind the bar in the public house that belonged to her family. At the back of the public house, in the middle of the stage there was a door. If you came directly through the door in the direction of the audience you would reach a trapdoor leading to the cellar that was just in front of the footlights. Shawn, who had the feeling that he was being chased by a terrifying man, came through the door, walking briskly and straight as an arrow towards the cellar, all the while talking quickly and incessantly, then lifted the trapdoor without interrupting his speech and disappeared abruptly into the cellar just as the door snapped closed. At the beginning of rehearsals the scene lacked tempo. Helene Weigel realised that there was simply too much text that didn't fit into the rhythm of the scene and told me to make cuts. Well, my part wasn't exactly big, so we had a row, which Helli ended up winning. This short appearance brought me a smashing success and was often followed by applause during the scene. Comedy had demonstrated how a pair of soiled trousers could take precedence over a text.

I / 10 / 11

SHAWN (*comes storming in*)   The queer dying fellow's beyond looking over the ditch and God help me he's following me now. *He disappears into the cellar.* [Synge, *The Playboy of the Western World*, original amended to reflect BE's cuts]

In the same piece there was also a scene during which Shawn's fear had to be overcome in a similarly controlled manner. Pegeen stood behind the bar as before. I stood beside her, next to an imaginary wall. Behind us was an extremely tall and narrow cabinet. Pegeen's father Michael and the titular hero, my rival, Christopher Mahon, the man who had killed his own father with a spade during a fight (played by the incredible Heinz Schubert) were also present. My Shawn valued dignity above all else in this conflict, in which everyone was against him. When things became threatening, and the 'father murderer' prepared himself for a fight, Shawn was suddenly no longer there, rather somewhere else entirely – on top of the cabinet to be exact. He stood on high, over the situation and his enemy, just as controlled and steady as before. You could say that he had risen above it all. The comical effect lay in the speed at which I climbed the cabinet. My climb was almost impossible to follow because I had had custom-built fixtures attached to the back of the cabinet, enabling me to get to the top almost in one leap, as if pulled up on a wire.

> SHAWN (*in great misery*)   I'd be afeard to be jealous of a man did slay his da.
> MICHAEL   Go on, you fool, and fight him now. (SHAWN *flees to the top of the cabinet.*)
> SHAWN   It's a queer story you'd go picking a dirty tramp up from the highways of the world.
> PEGEEN   Well, it'd be a poor thing to go marrying your like . . .
> CHRISTY (*with ferocity*)   Take yourself from this, young fellow, or maybe I'll add a murder to my deeds to-day. [Ibid., original amended to reflect BE's cuts]

In all the scenes or vignettes that I have described, comic effects were built into the performance through use of a consistent stance performed in front of an informed audience.

Linguistic Comedy:
Incongruity is to situational comedy as misunderstanding is to linguistic comedy. Of course, this misunderstanding is neither merely acoustic nor phonetic, nor the misunderstanding of circumstances in some other way. I also don't really mean simply pointing something out, or merely emphasising something drily, no matter how cleverly it is done. Rather, I'm talking about comedy that consists of taking surprising or astonishing stances in normal situations through gestural means, comedy that comes into being through startling insights in the course of normal conversation or discussion, insights that change the direction of

the conversation completely. Two jokes will make this point clear: two counterfeiters are sitting in the cell they share and talking. One says to the other: 'And imagine my surprise, my dear colleague, when I discovered one day that the government was printing the same money that I was!' In the other joke, a young man says to his girlfriend: 'Come on, let's take the short cut through the park.' To which she replies, 'No, today I really don't have the time.'

In Brecht's *Life of Galileo*, he describes Galileo in the following way during scene XIV:

> *1633–1642. A prisoner of the Inquisition,* GALILEO *continues his scientific studies up to his death. He manages to smuggle his principal work out of Italy.*
> *House in the country near Florence.*
> *A large room with a table, a leather chair, globe and small bed.* GALILEO *is old, ill and moves like a blind man.*
> ANDREA . . . a lot of people everywhere were hanging on your words and actions because they felt what you stood for was not a particular theory about the movements of the stars but the freedom to theorise in any field. Not just for any particular thoughts, in other words, but the right to think in the first place, which was now being threatened. So as soon as these people heard you recanting all you had said, they concluded that it was not merely certain thoughts about celestial motions that were being discredited but thinking itself that was being regarded as unholy, since it operates by means of causes and proofs.
> GALILEO (*pacing back and forth, after a pause*) So it is.

After this short line there was usually laughter. I didn't speak the line while pacing back and forth and after a pause, rather I spoke it quickly and directly, addressing the student's argument. I made it clear, almost eagerly, that Galileo's betrayal was a betrayal and would bring enormous consequences. Everyone was expecting regret for the situation Andrea had described. Disappointed, they laughed freely and involuntarily about the incredible cheek and

As Galileo, 1978 (photo by Vera Tenschert)

apparent intellectual casualness with which the perpetrator approached his crime.

GALILEO   In my view I have wrecked every experiment that might have been injurious to blind faith.

Brecht writes in 'Dialectics in the Theatre' ('Epic Theatre and Dialectical Theatre'):

Scenes take on either comic or tragic aspects; their tragic or comic side is worked out. This has little to do with the comic scenes that Shakespeare sprinkled throughout his tragedies (and, following him, Goethe in his *Faust*). Even the serious scenes can take on comic aspects (for example when Lear gives his kingdom away). Put more precisely, in such cases the comic aspect within the tragic scene or the tragic aspect within the comic scene emerges strongly as a contradiction. [Brecht, GW 16]

In *The Caucasian Chalk Circle*, the legal deliberations and decisions of Azdak, the village clerk, lend themselves to comedy, if they are played in a pointed way. Really, you shouldn't play down the comedic effects of this wonderful figure. Where things get vulgar, you needn't be unnecessarily concerned with depth.

LUDOVICA, *hips swaying, goes and picks up the knife.*
AZDAK *points at her.*
AZDAK: Do you see that? The way it sways? The criminal element has been discovered. The rape has been proved. . . . Do you imagine you can go around with a bottom like that and get away with it in Court? This is a case of deliberate assault with a dangerous weapon.

But even beyond that, Azdak's rulings, which spring from his own experience (earthy, casual and unjust as they are), must be taken more than anything as proof of intentions that are actually just. He manages to express his opinions a few times before the climax of the play, when he decides against the law but for justice. From the jumble of his judicial decisions:

AZDAK (*To the limping man*)   As compensation, you will receive a bottle of embrocation. (*To the blackmailer.*) You are sentenced to hand over half the proceeds of your deal to the Public Prosecutor, to keep the landowner's name secret. You are advised, moreover, to study medicine. You seem well suited to the profession. And you, Doctor, are acquitted because of an inexcusable professional mistake.

Of course clown scenes are comical. But a strict hierarchy ensures that every spectator knows which one of the clowns is to be viewed as more clever or stupid than the others. The ringmaster, frequently known as 'Herr Loyal', represents the pinnacle of erudition or pedantry; August, known among the people as 'the dumb one', is in the lowest position in the hierarchy, and the clown is in between. None of these three suffers from a lack of self-esteem and all of them require a partner to play off of. Most of the time, clowns are excellent acrobats or musicians – scenes made up purely of dialogue are less common.

In Tristan Rémy's collection *Clownnummern* [Clown Scenes] he describes a performance by the clown Dario/Bario, in which August, who can't figure out the solution to the riddle: 'It's not my brother, it's not my sister, yet it's still the child of my father and mother,' gets it from the clown:

Listen carefully. Because it's not my brother, not my sister either, but still the child of my father and mother . . . Well? Who is it? Why, it's me of course!

His adrenalin starts pumping immediately. He wants to make the ringmaster look like a fool by sharing this freshly acquired knowledge. The liveliness with which he presents himself to the others and puts himself at the centre of attention, in the bliss of understanding, complete with his new (falsely understood) knowledge, his strict and brisk rush towards the pre-programmed pratfall, catastrophe, or difficulty – all this makes a clown comical rather than ridiculous. This is an art unto itself. When the ringmaster immediately knows the correct answer to the eager August's question:

> It's not my brother . . . it's not my sister. And yet – yes, that's how
> it goes – it's still the child of my father and mother. Who is it?

August protests: 'Wow is he stupid. It's not me! . . .' and when Herr Loyal asks him: 'If it's not you, then who is it?' he points stubbornly to the clown: 'It's him! Dario!'

The spectators rejoice in the clown's perseverance in incompetence, his virtue in great measure but at a low, if also forgivable, level (an August is, after all, an August), and in his inability to understand the spectators' helpful cries (even the children's). In a film, I saw Dr Adrian Wettach, who performs alone as the clown Grock. He managed everything without speaking, but he had a problem that he tried to overcome through deliberation. He came on to the stage, hoping to play a very large grand piano, but he noticed after sitting down that his arms were too short to reach the keyboard. No matter what he tried in the next few minutes (and he had lots of intelligent ideas), he was still unable to overcome the distance. At the end of this impressive show, he came to the simple and not-so-obvious solution of pushing the grand piano closer to the stool with an enormous expenditure of energy. He now sat in the perfect position and the concert began. His exertion in executing his plan correctly, his movement technique and physical control were all intended to give the audience a giddy sense of superiority – one that it knew was only on loan from this great, clever and uproarious artist. Comedy seeks to draw the audience in and needs its reactions. Dramatic art, on the other hand, remains more distant, in order to make the suffering it portrays understandable, instead of generalising it.

Brecht, who in the twenties and early thirties called his type of theatre 'epic', a term which expressed his attitude towards both the new expressionistic and old naturalistic German theatre, later clarified this term, without disavowing it completely. A note about 'Epic Theatre and Dialectical Theatre' states:

Now we are attempting to make a transition from the *epic* theatre to the *dialectical* theatre. According to our opinion and intentions, the concept and practice of Epic Theatre were in no way undialectical; in the same way, a dialectical theatre will not be able to do without epic elements. [Brecht, GW 16]

In the practice of dialectical theatre, that is, during the rehearsals with Brecht, we were able to observe how he brought insights about reality into the subject matter of the play, in order to be able to work with this subject matter dialectically. We observed this process and had to swallow a lot of things which didn't appeal to us at first.

Being clever isn't important. Even originality isn't important. But doing without originality demands a bit of artistic daring . . . we have to ask those who are interested to be satisfied with the unordered pile of ideas and experiences that we impose on them. [Ibid.]

There was no theorising during Brecht's rehearsals. If you were interested, you could read the theoretical texts yourself and adopt them, to the extent that they were understandable. Brecht wasn't especially interested in interfering with our interests, or in energetically encouraging them. The few recommendations that he made were for the classical philosophers of dialectical materialism as well as their great successors and contemporaries. I assume he hoped that we would gain greater insight into social processes and deepen our acting philosophically. Back then, Professor Wolfgang Heise recommended that I read Marx's *Theses on Feuerbach*. He told me to simply read them as if they had been written for the theatre. I found it really astonishing how well they fitted, how I was able to take them directly and apply them to the theatre. From the eighth *Thesis on Feuerbach*:

Social life is essentially practical. All mysteries which mislead theory into mysticism find their rational solution in human practice and in the comprehension of this practice. [Marx, ibid.]

Later I wrote about Lenin's essay 'On the Question of Dialectics', which he wrote in Swiss exile. I can really recommend it – it's only five pages long. In the essay, Lenin talks about the two conceptions of progress that can be observed in history: the one, which the revolutionary does not share: 'development as decrease and increase, as repetition'; and the other, which appeals to him: 'development as a unity of opposites (the division of a unity into mutually exclusive opposites and their reciprocal relation)'.

The following passage proved instructive to my acting:

> The first conception is lifeless, pale and dry. The second alone furnishes the key to the 'self-movement' of everything existing; it alone furnishes the key to the 'leaps' to the 'break in continuity', to the 'transformation into the opposite', to the destruction of the old and the emergence of the new. [Lenin, 'On the Question of Dialectics']

I occupied myself with social theory [*Gesellschaftswissenschaft*] in order to transfer sociological concepts to the theatre, although the theatre is (or represents) a fictional reality. Every art form is fictional and illusory, and remains inconsequential outside itself. But inside this fiction – this assumed world that is totally created anew, this world that is created in the theatre and has nothing to do with reality except for taking its initial impulse from reality – inside this theatrical creation you can move about as if it were real, you can make use of natural laws and sociological descriptions of reality. Take note: every work of art, every successful theatre performance is a self-contained world (or to take it further: universe) and without presupposition when it comes to comparisons to or influences from the outside. It carries all justifications and truths within itself. That is the attractive freedom of art. If you're in any way interested in human or social concerns, if you bring them on to the stage and approach this enterprise fairly and honestly, all your good intentions and hard work amount to absolutely nothing in the end if you don't create theatre – that is, entertainment and pleasure beyond the expectations of a demanding audience.

Questions and Answers

Also participating: Barbara Brecht-Schall

QUESTION   Even if I didn't understand a word of the performance yesterday, I saw that the actors conveyed something – feelings and emotions, to be precise – as if they had been interpreting real people, still without empathy, but coming close to it.

ES   First of all, let me also say that Brecht's suggestions for the theatre in no way demand a certain style of acting, rather his suggestions or system are a method, that is, a process of working through roles. The final performance, in which you can detect a certain style, cannot be determined in advance. You never know where artistic work is going to lead you in the end; this is a risk you have to assume. Concerning your question: you are correct that the actors allow an interpretation to come through in their roles, thereby preventing empathy. For example, Franziska Trögner, who plays Grusha in *The Caucasian Chalk Circle*, always has to say to herself (and I support her in this): Grusha is not good, not good. That's simply not enough – she's tenacious, stubborn, orderly, rational and many other things besides. That she seems good to the audience is another matter entirely, one that should not especially interest us. It would be wrong, therefore, to act like she is overwhelmed by the child who the fleeing midwife lays in her arms, that she thinks 'this poor worm just has to be helped'. That would be goodness, but you could also call it stupidity. To play the scene in the right way you can only show that a burden, something disruptive, has been given to her or forced upon her: what should she do with it? From the beginning, she wants to get rid of the child, but situations keep occurring in which she must take the child out of danger, a little further each time. After a while, an unintentional bond is formed, she grows closer to the child – but not because she was predestined to do so as a good person, but because she can't escape helping him in certain necessary ways. Goodness wouldn't help her at all; rather, she must show the long road behind the two of them, the many difficulties along the way

129

and their solutions before she decides to be the child's mother. Without difficulties there can be no goodness (or something that can be described in that way) and no one gladly accepts difficulties – that is what must be shown.

It's the same way with all strong feelings. Pure feelings always come into friction with harsh reality (in life and on stage). To put it more clearly: most of the time they don't exist at all, and if they do, just for a short period of time. You have strong feelings for a girl, and what if she doesn't co-operate with them? That's really annoying. So, you don't have to pay special attention to a play's textual specifications (the meaning of which you must absorb intellectually), because the text's meaning expresses something pure, that is, it doesn't make for pleasurable theatre, as we understand it, if it is not reflected upon. Pleasurable theatre results from taking the meaning of a text and dealing with it within a situation, in giving or burdening the text with a layer of gestural meaning. Actually, in theatre no single thought exists solely in the spoken word, even if it is meant to. As it is brought across the stage, speaking only for its own content, its meaning changes when it comes into contact with the total interaction of different behaviours in the performance (the overall *Gestus*). This becomes clearer if we put it more simply or familiarly: a spoken 'yes' is, in reality, seldom a real, complete 'yes'. Let's say a girl is asked by a young man: do you love me? She loves him, but doesn't have the courage to tell him. So she answers with a 'no' in this case, meaning 'yes', and hopes that her sweetheart will understand. So she says 'no', and when she says 'no' it means 'no', but 'no' is 'yes'. That's what makes for the stance – it turns the meaning of the text round, alters every thought beyond recognition, yielding it recognisable in the end.

Let's look at a longer passage. *Life of Galileo* contains many passages in which Galileo discusses his views on reason. These passages are all beautiful and convincing, and make you eager to disseminate them, to align yourself with them. But if you take the story or the plot of the play and combine these phrases with the events in the play, you notice that the phrases become disharmonious, or in any case different. The story and reality are equally relevant to the spoken word; the only difference is that theatre takes place in an empty space, whereas reality is not to be trifled with. In both cases reality is malleable, able to be manipulated and restricted. In the third scene, at the beginning of the play, Galileo has a wonderful line to say to his friend Sagredo: 'Yes, I believe in reason's gentle tyranny over people. Sooner or later they have to give in to it.' If I speak this line in the way I just spoke it, without *Gestus*, the line is acceptable. But I, as an actor, know that this line is not true for Galileo during the plot of the play, that it is not generally valid, since he is battered and shaken by those in power because of his belief in reason, and finally gives up this belief. So I distance this phrase by speaking it in a way that the audience finds noticeably frivolous, almost thoughtless. [Demonstrated practically during the seminar.]

If the people down there say: 'Such a pretty phrase, and he says it so superficially. Why's he talking so strangely?' I've achieved what I wanted. I draw attention to the phrase, make it disreputable, and the audience is made aware of a contradiction between the meaning and performance. In principle, every stance that is taken on stage should be dialectically related to the actual meaning of the text. What is wished for or subjective must come into friction with the figure's actual behaviour, that which determines the figure and gives him contour. The demands of a figure, just like the demands of an actual person, are not met if you assume that there is no identity between demand and fulfilment, because both become a process that must be undertaken. I have to perplex people, make them aware of the way I conceive of the role.

QUESTION   What kind of stance does the actor take towards his figure? Does he have to think about it?

ES   I'm of the opinion that you shouldn't begin work on a role with preconceived moral judgements or specific ideas about your figure's character. The actor should think, and introduce the critique that he wants to apply to his role before the rehearsals.

This critique must be expressed mainly dramaturgically and its intentions clarified through changes in the plot. In this way the actor is later able to play his role and not the critique of his role, because the former must be meshed with the latter, in the manner described, that is, through precise determination of the sequence of stances. Only in this way can he defend his figure to the last (whoever it may be), even when the plot exposes his figure as a criminal or idiot. I've played Ui/Hitler, I've played Lenin, Oppenheimer and all kinds of other roles, and I've always defended my figures while I played them. Public opinion and my personal opinion played no role in this. World history judges political criminals themselves, not their opinions or preferences. Reactionaries are correct from their own point of view. Even if I think their point of view is incorrect, I can't play it as incorrect. Rather, I have to play it as the correct point of view for the person that I'm playing. The story and plot of the play in performance will expose the figures and their points of view to the audience's judgement.

QUESTION Have you always been successful?

ES I've walked down a long road lined with some of the worst critiques that you can get, but also some radiant reviews.

QUESTION How do you train for your roles? What do you have to pay attention to in order to be an actor like you?

ES I don't avoid difficult sequences of movement, risky falls, dance routines, songs and high notes, even if they lie at the outer limits of my ability. I work on them, that is, on the required condition and technique, I toil until I'm successful, until I get a grip on things or fail. But if I fail, then I fail well. I start concentrating on a big performance on the evening before it. The actual preparatory work (physical, vocal and breathing technique, text repetition) lasts between four and five hours. The distinguished actor Gustav Gründgens said once in a television interview (after he had decided to give up his profession and take a trip round the world) that his entire adult life had consisted of the day before *Hamlet* and the day after *Hamlet*, the day before *Faust* and the day after *Faust*. He wrote something similar on 14 July 1959 in Moscow to Alice and Christoph Bernoulli:

> I'm such a workaholic that I don't know how to live. I always find myself between one big premiere and another, and I'm unkind to the few friends that I have because I'm constantly overworked.
> [Gustav Gründgens. *Briefe, Aufsätze, Reden*]

I can relate to that. The Sisyphusian difficulty for such actors is not that they have to play the role so often, but rather that they have to make it seem like they are playing the role for the first time every time. They have to bring an improvisatory character to their performance, even if it's only simulated.

QUESTION   What was Brecht like?

BBS   May I say something, as long as I'm also sitting in front of this group of young people: please regard all anecdotes about my father with the utmost suspicion.

QUESTION   Another question concerning preparation. What do you do to eliminate certain labels? Actors who work according to Stanislavsky prepare themselves in exactly the same way. I don't think there's any difference.

ES   I think that real Stanislavsky actors tend less towards artistic or acrobatic theatre. When the Berliner Ensemble performed for the first time in Moscow, the Muscovites and our colleagues there were astonished because we reminded them of Meyerhold. Meyerhold, and others like Vakhtangov and Tairov behaved, differently from their teacher Stanislavsky. They advanced much more strongly into a fantastical world on stage and they didn't come to terms with many of the tenants of socialist realism. Meyerhold was later shot.

By the way, back to practical preparation: I've acted in many plays hundreds of times, in *Ui* more than 500 times, but it's not possible for me to perform without first having repeated the text thoroughly in advance in a time-consuming manner. And that applies not just to the words, but also the associated stances, walks, actions and reactions. I'm telling all of you: playing a protagonist is an extremely strenuous affair. I can only discourage you from doing it.

QUESTION   Are there many possible stances for a particular role?

ES   Personally I call the type of theatre I make polemical theatre. This means that I am interested in theatre at all (since I became an adult– earlier there were other reasons) because I can solve a problem in a satisfying way by means of the figure in the play, knowing that my opinion is not that of others, that my intelligence is limited and that the rightness of my thoughts is just as doubtful as those of my political opponents. I would always like to act with a kind of lightness (God knows that it does not come easy to me). This allows people to notice that I am standing behind the figure with my own intelligence and that the stances that I offer are stances among an endless number of possible ones, which they are free to accept or imagine. I would like to act in order to express: I have chosen this stance for this scene, you do not have to share it, you may join me but you don't have to. You are welcome here as long as the play lasts, even with views and stances that displease me. That is the difference in regard to the pure Stanislavsky actor, who aims at making his own characterisation the uniquely gratifying one. The offer I am describing asks the audience to participate. And when I succeed in this, I believe that my opinion contains all the other opinions for and against it that arise in the audience.

QUESTION   But I just want to know practically – how do you get there?

ES   How do I get to this point practically? I can only repeat what I have already said. I assume such a clear stance to my texts or to the situation in which I am acting that it becomes extreme to a point where the audience notices the discrepancy. And now the audience can enter the equation because textual meaning and the stance towards it, situation and the stance towards it do not imply and express the same thing, because the one plays on the other but the two are not mixed into a pudding. The audience enters the situation with an independent opinion, can find a voice, so to speak, even literally as far as I'm concerned. By means of a particular or conspicuous stance I turn over the text and with it the figure to the audience for evaluation and judgement.

QUESTION Did you start being an actor after you met Brecht? What did you do before? What have you performed that isn't by Brecht?

ES Shortly after the war I took acting lessons in the acting school attached to the Magdeburg Municipal Theatre. In 1948 I went to the Stadttheater in Frankfurt an der Oder. In fifty-one I went to Berlin, first to the Neue Bühne, then in fifty-two to the Berliner Ensemble. When I encountered Brecht, I had a completely different conception of the theatre from his (insofar as I can think today of a conception of theatre on my part at that time). In any case I was faced with people who had been educated and developed in a very different way from me. My wife [Barbara Brecht], whom I met at the time, was born in Berlin but spent her childhood and youth as an emigrant in other countries. I grew up, in contrast, in Germany during the Third Reich. What was to be learned at the Berliner Ensemble from the other colleagues – including anti-fascists who had been in concentration camps, prison and/or exile, related not only to the art of acting but also to life in general. When I was working with Brecht, I was not in a position to engage him. I was taught and was able to learn to the extent that I was willing. I was secretly convinced that we should have been playing much more expressive theatre than what I saw in the oppressive slowness of the *Mother Courage* production. At that time the only theatre that pleased me was the kind that excited and exhausted me within two hours; everything else left me indifferent, in particular the message. I had a long, thorny path before me, if we understand thorns to be painful crises, and Brecht was a master at pushing me into new crises. Seriously, he exorcised what he considered to be false (and much was), for my own good, I admit, but not always with my consent. He hated the relics of the past and the stumbling blocks (some the size of boulders) of the 1950s up until his death, and some, I among them, learned to understand this hatred.

BBS   We don't perform only Brecht at the Berliner Ensemble, that's a legend. It's true that we usually take Brecht plays with us when we go abroad, because that's what people want to see us perform. Around sixty per cent of our repertoire has always been by authors besides Brecht; it's the same at the moment. Not all our directors, the young ones included, produce plays in the way prescribed by Brecht. A few of them have taken very different paths.

QUESTION   Which authors' works do you like to perform the best?

ES   I've tried much too little. In a theatre like ours, where only three or four plays a year are produced, I don't get to play all the roles that I wish I could, and I've seen myself grow too old for a few that I would have liked to play. It would be weak opportunism if I were to name Brecht right now. It also wouldn't be true. Although I've acted in a few of his pieces happily all my life, there are a few other plays by other dramatists which I would have also gladly acted in. I went to the Theater im Palast in order to play Edgar, the commander of the fortress in Strindberg's *Dance of Death*. *Oedipus*, *Timon of Athens* and *Lear* excited me as well. I evaluate contemporary playwrights on a case-by-case basis.

QUESTION   Why were there changes to the text? I compared what you performed with the original.

BBS   A few lines were deleted, a few scenes were cut. Do you really want to sit in the theatre past midnight?

ES   Every director has the right to change the piece according to his conception of it. That is, he can cut lines and move scenes around. My text is exactly the way it was printed.

QUESTION   I have another question, concerning when you said that the audience should ask itself questions when an actor says something on stage. How?

ES   Yes, the actor would have to provoke these questions.

QUESTION   But that assumes that it's really possible to pass judgement on reality or on relations. These days that's very difficult. Not everything is black and white. Don't you think that in our contemporary situation, where nothing is black and white, you have to take other paths in order to do justice to reality, or maybe take a path in the same direction but one that is dramaturgically different? ES   Yesterday, we put on a specific play about a specific theme: *Life of Galileo*. And I would welcome it if I got my hands on a new play, about this or another theme, either surprising from a dramaturgical standpoint or conventional. And if this play were just as effective and enlightening as the one yesterday, I would perform it. The use of materialist dialectics in the theatre is only beginning. It's something new and far from exhausted. It will be present in world theatre, if at all, only after its way of thinking has also become part of our way of feeling, when you think self-evidently that way and every feeling gives rise to its respective anti-feeling. Anyone can have sympathy and actors don't dislike suffering on stage. But to me the better actor is the one who, while suffering, continuously integrates the opposite feeling into his performance as a matter of course, for example, hatred for the cause of the suffering. I grant you the fact that in capitalist countries international manipulation makes insight into social realities difficult or impossible. However, I think that the 'black and white' that you're missing is more clearly present now than in the past. Widespread misery, which, despite the high unemployment in the Federal Republic of Germany, is not yet visible on the streets, looms large in the slums of the countries that we call the poorhouses of the world.

QUESTION   How is theatre supposed to expose and condemn the causes of this situation? How is theatre even capable of doing that? ES   By using the right pieces. Unfortunately, Brecht died in fifty-six – much too early. But others are writing.

BBS   It would be great to have new pieces, but any given piece becomes a new piece each time it is performed. Take Ui, for example – he's played differently in different countries, and not always as Adolf Hitler. Each country has its own Arturo Ui.

QUESTION   Why is it that after Brecht's death there is no one, no dramaturg of his school, who is carrying on his ideas, the way it used to be, back when every thinker had a school to carry on his ideas after death? After all, Brecht was not only a dramatist, but also a thinker, a writer and a philosopher.

ES   After his return from emigration, Brecht encountered a generation of young Germans who were, in a certain sense, helpless, and desperately needed new thoughts and stimuli for new ways of thinking. Because our reserves of experiential knowledge had been more or less emptied, we were hungry for knowledge that had held its validity throughout the ages, and for the knowledge of the Resistance. We were intent on learning, we were students dependent on a remarkable teacher, in a way that is not common these days. No one could deny that he took on the character of an *Übervater*, albeit without smothering us. Although his directorial and literary attempts were not completely exemplary in a general sense, for many of us they were cogent, convincing, and with far-reaching consequences, resulting in a considerable series of duties and responsibilities that stretched into the next few decades. And for some of us, one duty became especially urgent with time: namely to be rid of this teacher, this know-it-all, who remained as intrusive as ever. Virgina, the daughter of the elderly, half-blind Galilei who is under house arrest, announces the arrival of a guest in the following manner:

> GALILEO   Is that Andrea?
> VIRGINIA   Yes. Shall I send him away?
> GALILEO (*after a moment*)   Show him in.
> VIRGINIA *brings* ANDREA *in.*
> VIRGINIA (*to the monk*)   He's harmless. Used to be his pupil. So now he's his enemy.

Even if this passage is from a different context, the rule remains the same: the teacher (even the beloved teacher) must be killed. In his *Maxims and Reflections* Goethe writes:

> The most terrifying thing for a student is that in the end he must assert himself against his teacher. The more powerful the teacher's

influence, the more distressed (or even despairing) is the student. [J. W. Goethe, *Maximen und Reflexionen*]

The student has to destroy the teacher within, or he will never be independent. This assassination is being worked at, of that I am certain. I can say humbly that those of us at the Berliner Ensemble have already taken a few steps in this direction, have lived and thought beyond what we learned from poor BB. The question of who will be successful in continuing the Brecht school with a new quality that is adequate to the old genius remains to be answered. But ideas like Brecht's will always find fruitful ground.

BBS I'm not so sure that when great people found schools, their schools ever live up to their great founders. Strehler had a school. Are there a lot of Strehlers in Milan now? But I can list off a whole heap of people who only became what they are today through Brecht and his school: dramaturgs, directors, actors and dramatists. Let's come to the last question.

QUESTION Since the Berliner Ensemble was designed by Brecht to be a theatre for freedom, polemics and discussion, does it have the independence it needs to perform autonomous work within the context of your Democratic Republic?

ES Yes, I'm of the opinion that we've reached a time of great stability for now, and that the most important people at the BE (not the majority) are first-class, bright and capable of political thought, and therefore I don't have any great concerns for the Ensemble's future work, at least in terms of its own responsibility and boldness.

BBS Could I just say one more thing? It wasn't an accident that Brecht went back to the area of Germany that would become the GDR. It wasn't that people were necessarily immediately enthused by his theatre, but they gave him a theatre, they gave him money, and the means to work. What more can you ask for?

QUESTION The Berliner Ensemble is known as a school, as a point of dissemination for Brecht. Is this an accurate reflection of reality?

BBS   Watch our performances and judge for yourself. We performed the *Chalk Circle*, we're performing the *Threepenny Opera* and in Rome we're going to perform *Galileo*.

ES   Our most recent premiere was Shakespeare's *Troilus and Cressida*.

BBS   There's a direct flight from Milan to Berlin.

We learned, that we should not
wallow in great pain but should show
the broken hearts and their breakers
over and over.

TEL AVIV SEMINAR
TEL AVIV 1989

During one of my trips to Israel, the University in Tel Aviv invited me to give a lecture. The comfortable hall was overflowing with students and interested listeners from the entire cultural scene.

Here, just like everywhere that I met curious people (whether they were curious but mistrustful, like the students in Oxford, or whether they falsely found me sympathetic to their cause, like the skinheads at Riverside Studios on the Thames, who saw a fellow skinhead in my portrayal of Ui/Hitler) there were conflicts and clarifications, but finally without much effort, also a certain productivity that was and is still possible at the theatre.

Ladies and gentlemen, I will speak about the art of acting. My experiences in the theatre have been many and varied, and I remain ambivalent about them up to the present day. Any accomplished actor should talk about what he really does on stage. If he's enthralled with metered language, he'll cultivate his voice in order to best convey verses and poetry. If he loves dramatic escalation, he'll cultivate this passion and only allow the intensity of human relationships to enter the foreground. If he loves tenderness and tears, he'll discover them everywhere, just like he who is cruel in the depths of his soul will reduce all human characteristics to these preferred dimensions. If he is a gifted dancer he will bring out rhythms and melodies that he finds in a particular piece. He who is in possession of this or that other talent must, provided that he does not give up the profession, decide if this handicap can be united with the best theatrical effects or if it only disturbs them. God knows that 'the pale cast of thought' is not helpful when an actor wants to uproot trees in his role, pluck stars from the sky for his lover, make utopian designs palatable, or simply sweep the spectators along, shock them or make them laugh.

For the moment, let's stick to the question of how intelligence and knowledge are used in the theatre, specifically in preparing and performing roles. My philosophical interest in plays and figures is part of my interest in materialist dialectics. In the list of contradictions in the sciences that Vladimir Illyich Lenin posited in his 1914–15 Bern essay 'On the Question of Dialectics', class struggle is the dialectic in social science that theatre urgently requires. This quote is a standard part of my seminars:

> In mathematics: + and −, differential and integral.
> In mechanics: action and reaction.
> In physics: positive and negative electricity.
> In chemistry: the combination and dissociation of atoms.
> In social sciences: class struggle.

Here I have to note that Lenin is not referring exclusively to a revolutionary process, rather to ever-present conflicts and developments or the continuous daily struggle, brought about by the incompatible needs of separate classes, a struggle which results through a reciprocal friction or movement, which Lenin meant as a notice-taking and working-out of social contradictions. This list seems to be correct, at least in my own experience, and is systematically formulated. To this extent dialectic in the theatre has to be conceived of sociologically (in a figurative sense and certainly not in an agitatory sense). But real class struggle is not just openly revolutionary. A contradiction is not always clear, antagonistic and easily recognised as such by everyone, and is by no means a polarity. Class struggle can also take a concealed, weaker form (and actually quite often does). It can become ordinary; you can get so used to it that you no longer notice the mistakes or the incorrect behaviour that have insinuated themselves. It can happen that you can no longer differentiate between resistance and oppression because they have both been shrouded in a comfortable satisfaction that seems to unite them good-naturedly. But these shrouded contradictions have to be uncovered for the audience. Brecht made many suggestions for how to describe reality through contradictions on the stage. For those contradictions which have become obscured due to familiarity, he suggests the *Verfremdungseffekt*. Through the use of this effect routine behaviour, which is inhumane or unworthy of a human being can be made unfamiliar once again, so that the behaviour may be recognised by the audience for what it really is, for 'something else', something erroneous, degenerate, sclerotic, thoughtless or even magnificent, astonishing and many other things besides. People often forget that you can also take behaviour which is humane or worthy of a human being, and make it seem strange and thereby more easily recognisable. Irrespective of all this, Brecht never tired of pointing out that all contradictory human interaction should be represented in a suitably contradictory manner. Personally, I would define the contradiction that the actor has to find in the plot and between figures and bring it to the fore in this way:

> A contradiction is a unity of an individual claim and actual behaviour and action, it is the unity of the subjective plan and its actual execution as influenced and corrected by the objective world, between wish and experience. At the theatre, the objectivity represented by the sum of the incidents on stage takes the place of the objective world.

Let's begin with simple acting, with the non-dialectical kind. It hasn't simply been done away with. It remains the norm on our stages and it's even tenable if sublated in a dialectical environment, one that has been prepared dramaturgically with certain pre-conditions. Just like history renders a verdict on those acting within history, so are verdicts about figures rendered not only by actors through their roles, but also through the dramaturgy that is inherent to or imposed upon a particular performance. If a single, penetrating contradiction is so strongly positioned dramaturgically that it cannot be repressed or overcome through the basic premises of the plot, the figures themselves can be sublated in this basic contradiction to the point that they can do without any additional *Verfremdung* in some of the scenes.

Bertolt Brecht built one such contradiction into his *Fatzer* fragment and held it through to the end: one social formation is left behind for ever, while its structures of power and persecution simultaneously live on. A theme for the century. If the dialectic is present strongly enough in the dramaturgy of the scene, the actor can treat both text and *Gestus* (his stance towards the text) almost equally, that is, he doesn't have to influence one with the other. As far as I'm concerned he can also act with empathy, that is, bring text and stance close together, try to synchronise them. Then political or moral statements don't have to be performed in a special way, they can be played simply. For example: in *Fatzer*, Fatzer gives his comrades with whom he has deserted an ultimatum.

FATZER

do you really want to know? now
i challenge you to join
this fight that I have here
and come back here tonight at the same time
to the same place where you failed, so that
we can look each other in the eye again and
so i can beat those
who have beaten me!

KOCH

i'm astonished. honestly:
we thought you would to tell us
how
we could find meat.

i thought we want to get some meat, not fight.

FATZER

honestly: i thought we
wanted to fight.

KOCH

that's strange. but if you insist,
we'll have to vote on it . . .
well then: do you want to
get some meat or fight?

KAUMANN

get meat.

BÜSCHING

meat.

KOCH

well then, first we get some meat. we've voted, fatzer. the
fight's off. [Brecht, *Fatzer*. Spielfassung des Berliner Ensembles]

Two decisions are juxtaposed, with no ifs, ands or buts:

1. If you leave a war in order to survive, you also don't want to die
of hunger
2. If you leave a 'dirty' war, you have to keep fighting against it,
even if you starve in the process.

Fatzer is outvoted. Now he curses his comrades and shows them
his contempt. This contempt may be presented as contempt.

FATZER

i'm against your mechanical way
because a man's not a lever.
also i have a great aversion to doing only those deeds
that are useful to me among many others.
but desire to bury the good meat and spit
in the drinking water
that's not easy.
your unhealthy desire to be like cogs
but I don't want to . . .

As Fatzer in Brecht's Demise of the Egoist Johann Fatzer
(adapted by Heiner Müller), 1978 (photo by Vera Tenschert)

gauge my abyss
keep of me only what is useful to you
the rest is fatzer. [Ibid.]

Natural feelings of human dignity and its painful limits should provide a justification for moving beyond themselves. They should be
expropriated, so that they may be developed or reshaped into
human energy or strength for the struggle. Fatzer leaves his
comrades in order to assert himself more as an individual, to fight
for his own cause through himself. In a monologue, he announces:

FATZER

the air and the streets belong to all humans
i must be allowed to move freely in the stream of people,
hear human voices, see human faces . . .
                                    even in battle i have to breathe
eat and drink like always, maybe it will last for ever,
that is, longer than i will and then if i am killed
i will not have lived . . .
                                    that all proves that i can walk
where i want and how i want. [Ibid.]

Persisting in order to still your hunger or persisting in order to starve
deliberately but independently – both of these are honourable
motives. But one of them is less correct if the other is more correct,
for the material is not a priori more urgent than the ideal, just the
ideal does not, in and of itself, have more historical potential than the
material. Both concepts remain relative (and rightly so), equally
justified in defence of their respective claims and in this way push
forward towards a dialectical resolution within the performance. A
scene, if staged in this way, doesn't need to emphasise or work out
the main contradiction between the persecuted and the persecutors.
No figure in the scene can halt the precarious motion of the sword
of Damocles that hangs above them. Fatzer's own persecuted
comrades have to be the ones to prevent him, who is also

persecuted, from striking out on his own, because he could betray their hiding place and the fact of their desertion to their counter-revolutionary pursuers. He would be risking the destruction of the entire community to which he belongs with his own person. It is therefore logical that his comrades beat him. On the one hand we have his original intention, on the other, what remains of this intention, that is, the corrected or revised intention. Taken together, these two make up the social contradiction that has to be portrayed in the theatre. But the actor shouldn't interpolate his own critique on to Fatzer when he forms his intentions.

In the same way, Fatzer's critique of his comrades (who are in the right) and his grand ideas about the rights of the individual should be acted and spoken with conviction, in all the absoluteness and beauty that many see in them, in a measure equal to their danger and falsity for the miserable social milieu he finds himself in. Out of all of this should come the insight that humans shouldn't have to change; society should change first. The only possibilities that the individual has for free or restricted personal development are the ones provided or allowed by society. In every oppressive society, the assertion of an individual's rights entails the misfortune of others to the extent it is successful. The scene can be played in this way: Fatzer is correct, his words are wise, he is brave and unflinching in his convictions. Koch, Kaumann and Büsching are correct, their words are wise, they are brave and unflinching in their convictions. The performances need not be distanced because the scene itself accomplishes this when viewed in the context of the entire play.

Fatzer is a play about the search for free space and, because no one freely gives up space, it is also necessarily a play about escalating expropriations: each acquisition, each gratification of desire, each bite and sip is an appropriation, an act of violence and chaos without an end in sight. A scene supported by the proper dramaturgy can in many cases reduce the dialectic shown by the actors. But an actor should consent to this only rarely, never when he gets the urge to grab the contradictions by the collar and, following Marx, make relations dance and play. I believe that the following lines from Marx in his introduction to 'Critique of Hegel's Philosophy of Law' are an ode to theatre, and not only to German theatre. They are recorded here thanks to the help of Prof. Dr Heinrich Gemkow, who found the quote for me:

> The point is not to allow the Germans a minute for self-deception and resignation. The actual pressure must be made more pressing by adding to it the consciousness of pressure . . . These petrified relations must be made to dance by singing their own tune to them! The people must be taught to be terrified at itself in order to give it courage. This will be fulfilling an imperative need for the German nation, and the needs of the nations are in themselves the ultimate reason for their satisfaction. [Marx, *Collected Works 3*]

It's fun to make contradictions clear without having to caricature them. I quote from the *Philosophisches Wörterbuch* [Dictionary of Philosophy] by Georg Klaus and Manfred Bahr:

> The essence of the concept of dialectical development is expressed in the three *basic laws of the dialectic*: 1. *The law of the unity and the 'struggle' of opposites*, which states that an entity's inherent dialectical contradictions are the driving force of every movement and development, meaning that movement is conceived of as self-movement. 2. *The law of the transformation [Umschlagen] of quantitative into qualitative changes* and vice versa, which conceives of development not as simple quantitative change or evolution, but emphasises the unity of quantity and quality, of evolution and revolution, continuity and discontinuity within development. 3. *The law of the negation of the negation*, according to which every development is a higher development, not a simple destruction of the old, rather a process of dialectical negation, during which earlier stages are overcome while their positive and developable aspects are simultaneously preserved.

In the third scene of *Life of Galileo*, I find an incident appropriate to the first law, that is, a clear contradiction between text and *Gestus*, which is in this case a frivolous approach to the stance taken towards the text. In this hymn of praise to reason, Galileo grants reason the primary place among all other means of convincing people; in fact, he practically deifies it. He overestimates the uselessness of not yielding in the face of evidence. And in doing so, he creates his own enemy. The phrase 'evidence is not evidence if it is not accepted as evidence' is just as valid in its reverse formulation, which is illustrated by Uriah in *Man Equals Man* while he stands before a pathetic mock-up of an elephant:

> URIAH He'll take it for an elephant all right, let me tell you. He'd take this beer bottle for an elephant if somebody points at it and says: I want to buy that elephant.

The figure Galileo does not understand that reason [*Geist*] is not a kind of greatness that need merely be employed to be effective. Rather it relies on an entire framework of other factors beyond the initial realisation that it provides, each factor in its own time, if it is to be acknowledged, let alone tolerated or even admired. These factors include acquiescence, permission, meekness, humility, subservience, considerateness, patience, caution, conformity (today opportunism) guaranteed impunity and many others. With his telescope Galileo made a discovery that will revolutionise the Ptolemaic conception of the solar system. He trusts that anyone who wants to can confirm his discovery by looking through the new telescope. 'It has been proven,' he says and trusts in human reason, and in doing so only thinks of those who agree with him. He forgets about the rulers, he factors them out of his thinking. He doesn't waste a single thought on those for whom his discovery could be dangerous, on those for whom it comes at an inopportune time or for whom it doesn't fit. It is my job to portray this contradiction between Galileo's unconditional belief in the results of reason (and in reason itself), and his incorrect and naive appraisal of the interests of the powerful. Therefore I speak the text I have at my disposal (as far as my stance towards the text is concerned, not the actual meaning of the text) not as intelligently as I really believe it to be, but rather frivolously and superficially in light of the play's conditions and their accompanying dangers. I do this in order to provoke the spectators, who are really only trying to follow my arguments. No human warmth, no cleverness, no ingenious flights of fancy can escape subordination to the stance.

> GALILEO   I'm not talking about their shrewdness. I know they call a donkey a horse when they want to sell it and a horse a donkey when they want to buy. That's the kind of shrewdness you mean. But the horny-handed old woman who gives her mule the extra bundle of hay on the eve of a journey, the sea captain who allows for storms and doldrums when laying in stores, the child who puts on his cap once they have convinced him it may rain: these are the people I pin my hopes to, because they all accept proof. Yes, I believe in reason's gentle tyranny over people. Sooner or later they have to give in to it . . . Thinking is one of the chief pleasures of the human race.

The first law of the dialectic offers or asserts itself often, allowing a playful mood to break out on stage, a mood that mimics life in all its fullness and lacks nothing compared to real life except that it is not real and therefore inconsequential. However, this fictional life allows us to understand the joyful or triumphant feelings of explorers, lovers or mass murders, whether or not they turn out to be well founded. But before all consideration of or ideas about a role, there is a certain primordial fear (which is simultaneously a primordial hope) that hangs on you like a belt of lead weights, and calls into question your ability to stand before people and present an intimate or public action which you've never experienced, in all its precision and awkwardness, exact in detail yet chaotic. This fear feeds an actor's every expression when he's standing out there on stage. He can really make a fool of himself if he can't make himself and his audience forget the far-fetched nature of his task, without chutzpah and never shamelessly. Once in Babelsberg the actor Wolf von Beneckendorff told me as we sat across from each other in the dressing rooms at seven in the morning being made up: 'It's times like these that make you realise that this is no profession for grown-ups.' He was right. But you have to decide for yourself what happens before you step on to the stage.

I'd like to present an example of the second law of the dialectic: in *The Caucasian Chalk Circle* the intentions and world-view of a character are radically changed for the better, socially and morally speaking, from one moment to the next, without preparation. Something like that doesn't happen very often in dramatic literature. The poor man's judge Adzak bends the law to help the poor, which amuses the audience and becomes a matter of course. But his final judgment in the quarrel of two women over a child is totally unexpected, for all other figures and for himself. It is not Solomonic, it requires no wisdom, but rather comes into being through a new experience that causes a new insight, brings about a new sort of discernment. Dialectically speaking, you could call it 'the transformation from quantitative to qualitative change' as already described here, where quality and quantity are conceived of as a unity, just as evolution and revolution, continuity and discontinuity require each other. In the Bible, in 1 Kings 3:23–27, King Solomon judges a similar case in the following manner:

23. Then the king said, 'The one says "This is my son that is alive, and your son is dead"; and the other says 'No, but your son is dead, and my son is the living one.'"

24. And the king said, 'Bring me a sword.' So a sword was brought before the king.

25. And the king said, 'Divide the living child in two, and give half to the one, half to the other'.

26. Then the woman whose son was alive said to the king, because her heart yearned for her son, 'Oh my lord, give her the child, and by no means slay it.' But the other said 'it shall be neither mine nor yours; divide it.'

27. Then the king answered and said, 'Give the living child to the first woman, and by no means slay it; she is its mother.'

The judgment in Brecht's play is not wise in the same way, and it is also not a simply natural one, but rather one derived from social conditions and nevertheless touching in a human way.

> ADZAK   Plaintiff and defendant! The Court has listened to your case, and has come to no decision as to who the real mother of this child is. I as Judge have the duty of choosing a mother for the child. I'll make a test. Shauva, get a piece of chalk and draw a circle on the floor. (*Shauva does so.*) Now place the child in the centre. (*Shauva puts Michael, who smiles at Grusha, in the centre of the circle.*) Plaintiff and defendant, stand near the circle, both of you. (*The Governor's Wife and Grusha step up to the circle.*) Now each of you take the child by a hand.

I play it like this: Azdak speaks clearly to Grusha; he gives her a signal, a well-meaning piece of advice: you, as a maid, are the stronger one. Take your child!

> The true mother is she who has the strength to pull the child out of the circle, towards herself.
>
> THE SECOND LAWYER (*quickly*)   High Court of Justice, I protest! I object that the fate of the great Abshvili estates, which are bound up with the child as the heir, should be made dependent on such a doubtful wrestling match. Moreover, my client does not command the same physical strength as this person, who is accustomed to physical work.

Azdak shares this opinion and finds:

> AZDAK   She looks pretty well fed to me. Pull!

After a long tug-of-war between the two women, with a great expenditure of force on both sides, the Governor's Wife pulls

> the child out of the circle to her side. GRUSHA *has let it go and stands aghast.*
>
> THE FIRST LAWYER (*congratulating the Governor's Wife*)   What did I say! The bonds of blood!

AZDAK (*to* GRUSHA)   What's the matter with you? You didn't pull!
GRUSHA   I didn't hold on to him.

His favoured candidate has failed, even though he'd made it so easy for her. He hands the child to the Governor's Wife and announces out of nowhere:

Well then, we'll do the test once more

And says threateningly to Grusha:

so that I can be absolutely certain. (*Both women take their places once more.*)
AZDAK   Pull! *Grusha lets the child go once again.*
GRUSHA (*in despair*)   I raised him! And now I'm supposed to tear him apart? I can't do it.

This is the pivotal moment: the insight hits Adzak like a load of bricks. Speechless, eyes wide open in astonishment, he doesn't understand what he is in the process of comprehending. As he stands, he hears himself say:

And in this manner the court has established the real mother. (*To Grusha.*) Take your child and be off with it. I advise you not to stay in town with him.

Up to this point the trial has been a shameless fraud. But suddenly Azdak recognises that there is more to justice than the mere representation of class interests. Grusha forces him to not only to pass judgment (which he does gladly, with every privilege of his class) but rather to practise justice, which for him is total nonsense, a superfluous luxury. Azdak decides not in favour of the child and its mother, but rather in favour of the child and what it needs in its helplessness and vulnerability, namely mothering, which it hasn't received from its biological mother during the course of the play. The child is given over to its mother, in this case, its foster-mother. In order to present the contradiction between the process of passing judgment and Azdak's final judgment, it must be shown that Azdak is following neither the path of wisdom, which he couldn't care less about, nor the path of justice, which doesn't exist for him and people like him, and therefore for no one else either. He wants to give Grusha the child because he doesn't like the Governor's Wife, so he puts on a meaningless hocus-pocus. Nothing can go wrong because Grusha, who has always performed manual labour, is the stronger of the two. But Grusha misses her chance to take advantage of the situation not because she doesn't want to be party to judicial fraud, but because she persists in what for her is everyday humanity, and therefore troublesome: namely, not harming other people. In doing so, she stubbornly steers a surprised Azdak away from an almost-legal judgment and back towards a renewed type of illegality, to a new judgment, which is intentionally false, but nevertheless appears right to me (and many others). A lax and unprofessional trial leads to an incorrect and arbitrary judgment, which is or appears to be the only just one, given Grusha's relationship with the child.

Only now in 1997 at my home in Buckow have I decided to add a discussion of the third law of the dialectic, after looking through the manuscripts of previous seminars. Why didn't I do this before? Well, perhaps because I was in a hurry, was being lazy, superficial or absent-minded – certainly also because I didn't necessarily want to proceed systematically. There were examples for the third law: in Vsevolod Vishnevski's *Optimistic Tragedy* there's the liquidation and integration of the anarchists by the commissar, the party group and their sympathisers, in *Ui* there's the intimidation and incapacitation of the Cauliflower Trust and the vegetable sellers, later the take-over of the entire cities Capua and Cicero by Ui and his gang with the help of those that they bribed or strong-armed; practical negations of existing structures and pre-existing or recently-formed groups with their own special interests. The oversimplified yet much-touted casual connection between capitalism and communism derived from this law did not appeal to me: namely that the latter is victorious, the former in decline. This casual connection is often simplified even further in other plays and through other characters. I wasn't concerned with mechanical contradictions.

Doing nothing is still doing something: this thought is enlightening, but the dialectic does not concern itself with absolutes or mere thoughts – the negation of the negation can be experienced and performed, it pulls victims and perpetrators after it, it brings dramas and poems into being, symphonies and songs, frescos and monuments, printed and erased biographies. Relativised horrors, anachronistic conditions, existing centres of power, the masses and their leaders who have partially become anonymous, those who harm the existing order and those who protect it, revolutionary units and heavily armed armies – all of these must be reckoned with or against each other.

In Heiner Müller's *Germania 3*, Hitler appears to Stalin as Stalin is describing his own crimes. Stalin despises Hitler's crimes to the extent that they are dangerous to him and he promises Hitler an ignoble fate. That's the set-up in Müller's text – a scene with imaginary interlocutors (except for the soldier who delivers a report). Afterwards, Stalin sits again at his normal place and smokes his pipe, playing the 'Uncle Joe' that the Americans liked to see in him during the war. He implies that he intends to survive, and that despite the hatred and threats, he could represent 'the development of a higher development' not just a 'simple destruction' of the festering sore that is Nazi Germany. Evil will force an even greater evil to its knees. When something unacceptable struggles against or even defeats something even less acceptable, a positive outcome results. This outcome allows that which remains to appear positive in two respects: as the surviving better condition and as a victor over the unacceptable. The defeat of a great horror remains a great success, even when the lesser horror continues to exist.

II *Tank Battle*

Kremlin. Stalin drinking.

STALIN

Comrade, why are you drinking in the night?

What do you have to fear where your power is the law?
I know something about each man that is enough to kill
him . . .
I fertilised this land with blood
with human bodies
my bone-mills ground out an industry
I, the Great Stalin, leader of peoples.
I am the bloodhound.

OFFICER

The Germans are attacking, Comrade Stalin . . .

STALIN

I should have known, should have been the first to know.
And I stand naked before his divisions
My army headless . . .
Why the cold sweat on my brow.
Forgot who I am. The Great Stalin
I'm afraid of my own shadow.

HITLER, *bellowing a speech.*

STALIN

Hitler, my friend of yesterday. Brother Hitler.
Burn my villages. That is good.
They'll love me because they hate you . . .
Keep winning, push your tanks into the snow
That will bury them, when the time comes.
You'll see Moscow from a rat-cage
Ere our enemies are resurrected.

As I said before, after the threats of destruction, the prophecies of doom, father Stalin sits in his chair, sucking on his pipe like in the famous photo, and Moscow, the heart of the proletarian world, capital of the fatherland of all workers and the target of the Nazi army, can rest easy, for a light is burning in the Kremlin.

'Historical experience indicates', says order number fifty-five, which Stalin signed on 23 February 1942, 'that the Hitlers come and go, but the German people and the German nation remain.'

US senator Morgenthau, on the other hand, suggested that the Allies ban all industry in Germany and reduce the country to the level of an agrarian state. This reckoning with the past wasn't intended to be a 'process of dialectical negation' 'in which previous stages are overcome' (that is, the stages of barbarism, carried out or supported by countless Germans, both civilian and military) but whose 'positive and developable aspects are simultaneously preserved'.

The quintessence of the scene just described remains this: the figure Stalin will defeat (or negate) the Nazi horror, doing the world a great service in the process, even saving Europe. The fact that this service is also a horror that must be negated is another story. And, in reality, this scene in the Berliner Ensemble's 1996 production ends only with Müller's text, and not with a prognosis, conclusion or the hint of some sublation of this terrible contradiction. Müller's late works are deeply undialectical. He is a passionate storyteller, a recorder of crass contradictions. The political situation in Germany today is also one of stasis, without serious movement, and this condition is mirrored in the minds of many, both normal people and dramatists. Static times are met with static plans. A static condition does without dialectic until it is no longer tolerable. In this way many things detrimental to dialectics converge. In contrast, even the title of Brecht's *The Resistible Rise of Arturo Ui* proves itself to be friendly to dialectical thought; it provides a contradiction that both invites and demands a dialectical approach. The dialectical partner of the title is the story itself.

Back to the old manuscript. Let's talk about something else: dramatic representation, dramatic expression – what is it and how do we arrive at it? I started as a very young man. During my childhood I barely visited the theatre. *Peterchens Mondfahrt* [Little Peter's Trip to the Moon, Gert von Bassewitz], *Robert und Bertram*, *The Broken Pitcher* [Kleist], and one opera, *Der Waffenschmied* [The Weapon Smith, Albert Lortzing], are the only performances I can remember attending. Bombs destroyed the Magdeburg Stadttheater, the Wilhelmtheater and the Centraltheater. After the war a few makeshift playhouses scattered around the suburbs were erected, and the real city theatre for large operatic and dramatic productions opened in the former Gesellschaftshaus called 'Harmonie', near the completely destroyed city centre. It was here that I happened to see Friedrich Hebbel's *Gyges and his Ring* some time in either 1945 or 1946. Right at the beginning of the performance, when Romano Merck, playing Candaules, stepped out from behind a Dorian column and said:

> CANDAULES Today, you'll see the best of Lydia! [*Three Plays by Hebbel*, trans. Marion W. Sonnenfeld]

I saw my path in life stretching out clearly before my eyes. I was on the edge of my seat for the rest of the performance. I was excited to no end by the king, who, bragging about his wife's beauty, arranges for his young friend Gyges to see her naked (with the help of a ring that makes its wearer invisible), and by his humiliated, injured wife (just like in every play by Hebbel), who avenges her honour bloodily and decisively. I ran home, procured a copy of the play and memorised it word for word, from the first line above to the last lines that Rudophe says to Gyges after she has taken revenge on her spouse:

> I'm purified at last
> For only he who may has looked at me,
> But now I thus (*She stabs herself.*)
> divorce myself from you! [Ibid.]

After memorising the play, I ran to Romano Merck's house, which was near the city's glacis, rang the doorbell and demanded from the astonished man who opened the door to find me, a tyke in short trousers, the chance to recite the play. I declaimed as long as he let me and from that day forward I had acting lessons, first with him and later, after I had been accepted by the acting school at the association of city theatres, with Erwin Dorow, Otto Preuß,

Barbara Bufe and others. My parents had nothing against this.
Other children took piano lessons or played football; their son
took acting lessons. They didn't take my decision especially
seriously and certainly didn't see acting as a future career for me. I
also didn't think about acting as a possible career. I wasn't really
looking to start a career back when I was taking acting lessons, I
just wanted to become an actor. And besides, I was still at school.
I learned to love the written word, Hebbel's writing more than
anything else, which became my first love both because of Gyges's
story about the ring and because of one particular garland of
words, a cascade of letters, a fifteen-line stanza, which is one of the
most beautiful in all of dramatic literature:

GYGES   If the Castilian spring
     From which the fav'rites of the gods do drink,
     Which gleams with play of colourful reflection
     As though it had been strewn by Iris' hands
     With rainbows plucked apart, now if this spring
     Which had its origins on Mount Parnassus
     Is dulled by a thrown stone, it starts to rush
     And, wildly rushing, rises heavenward.
     And then, no nightingale, no lark can sing
     On earth, and, there up high, the sacred choir
     Of muses becomes silent too, and then
     True harmony can not return until
     A raging stream will grind the brazen one
     Into its darkest depths. And this compares
     To what occurs inside a woman's soul. [Ibid.]

   Christian Dietrich Grabbe also appealed to me. The fact that a
thirty-five-year-old poet could put the line '– Dark Pilot, who are
you –' [Christian Dietrich Grabbe, *Sämtliche Werke in vier
Bänden*, 3] in the mouth of his character Hannibal, in 1835, a year
before his own death, took my breath away. How could the highly
lauded yet worn-out classics compare? I was still at school, at the
Cathedral and Monastery Gymnasium on Augustastraße. I quit

before finishing, because the many roles that I had learned in the meantime didn't earn me any high marks and actually diminished my performance in some subjects. Besides that, I was first engaged as a certified official actor in Frankfurt an der Oder (far away from my mother) on 1 May 1948, in the same year I should have finished school. I regretted not finishing, but I never regretted starting my career as early as I did. Back then in Magdeburg I was a dreamer, still bursting with pubescent power. I devoured, ruminated on and excreted dramatic texts. I ate them up like raw flesh, without pondering their literary merits, solely for the purpose of absorbing them and then expelling them in someone else's presence, anyone's, although I also shouted them to the rooftops when I was alone. I thought of myself as a valve between the texts and the world. Only years later did I learn any kind of professionalism. In the rubble world of those years, the spoken word was for me a carnal, reflexive type of pleasure. I gobbled words down, savoured them as delicacies, then spat them out, casting them about me like pearls before swine. There was never any real thought in this; my elementary, erotic approach to texts was never disturbed by any specific intention. This approach was right in its way. What did I care about the figure Romeo, or the entire play *Romeo and Juliet*? But I loved the monologue in which the deeply hurt young man breaks out in a passionate and glowing song of praise for Juliet, demonstrating his longing for her. *This* expressed what I felt.

Romeo and Juliet, by William Shakespeare

Act II, Scene II

ROMEO

He jests at scars that never felt a wound.

(*Enter* JULIET *above at her window.*)

But soft, what light through yonder window breaks?

It is the east, and Juliet is the sun.

Arise, fair sun, and kill the envious moon,

Who is already sick and pale with grief

That thou, her maid, art far more fair than she.

Be not her maid, since she is envious;
Her vestal livery is but sick and green,
And none but fools do wear it; cast it off.
It is my lady, O, it is my love!
O that she knew she were!
She speaks, yet she says nothing; what of that?
Her eye discourses, I will answer it.
I am too bold, 'tis not to me she speaks.
Two of the fairest stars in all the heaven,
Having some business, do entreat her eyes
To twinkle in their spheres till they return.
What if her eyes were there, they in her head?
The brightness of her cheek would shame those stars,
As daylight doth a lamp; her eyes in heaven
Would through the airy region stream so bright
That birds would sing and think it were not night
See how she leans her cheek upon her hand!
O that I were a glove upon that hand,
That I might touch that cheek!

Back then in acting school we didn't work on individual roles.
We met with our teachers one-on-one, either in a vacant practice
space in the 'Harmonie' or at one of their homes, and worked on
a monologue or a longer passage in a single scene that had been
restricted to a single role, always without a partner. The passages
we worked on were well known in theatre circles and were
calculated to show off our brilliance, to make an impression when
we declaimed them in front of the director or other students. We
wanted to be admired, to blaze trails, to chart the territory in
which we hoped to move and conquer the area we had laid claim
to. We were trained for declamation, not for actual performance
in the theatre, and any performances that we saw seemed to have
come into being as if by immaculate conception – in any case we
hadn't a clue how a conglomeration of single texts out of a book
could come together and be transformed into a diverse, colourful,

dynamic collective work. The show-off pieces that I had in my 'audition box' (as we called it), were:

Kosinsky's passionate lovelorn tale from *The Robbers* by Friedrich Schiller:

KOSINSKY   Let me tell you, then, that I come of a noble family in Bohemia, and through my father's early death inherited a sizeable estate. My lands were like a paradise – for they contained an angel – a girl with all the charms that the bloom of youth can endow, and chaste as the light of heaven. [Schiller, *The Robbers and Wallenstein*, trans. F. J. Lamport]

Mortimer's tale about his time in Rome in Schiller's *Maria Stuart*:

At twenty years of age, your majesty,
Brought up to serve in strict obedience,
And taught to hate all taint of Popery,
I found my heart consumed with longing for
The lands of Europe. So I left my country,
Its gloomy Puritan conventicles,
And sped through France to Italy, the land
Of my desires, of which I heard such praise.
[Schiller, *Mary Stuart*, trans. F. J. Lamport]

Weißlingen's page Franz's surprise greeting in Goethe's *Goetz of Berlichingen*:

FRANZ   God's greeting, my noble Lord! I bring so many messages that I scarcely know how to begin. Bamberg and its environs for ten miles around send you a thousandfold: God's greeting! [Goethe, *Collected Works 7*]

Jacob's evening-star tale from Max Halbe's *Der Strom* [The Current], that ends:

JACOB (*proudly*)   Yes, my star won!
RENATE   And Heinrich's star?
JACOB   His came out only much later! A black cloud lay over his

star and didn't want to move away. And *my* star still sparkled and twinkled in the west! [Max Halbe, *Der Strom*]

These emotional recitations meant everything to us. We represented no one but ourselves; we played ourselves alone. We intended nothing less than to break open the floodgates of our spectators' hearts and minds, yielding them defenceless in the face of our onslaught. As I wrote in 1947 in *A Philosophy of Acting*:

> Do you not notice how your gurgling becomes ineffective, if it is not saturated with the lust of a boy entwined [*verkrallt*] with a woman for the first time? Art must overpower all humanity, in the small representative sample of an audience.

We (that is, a group of us in acting school) were so convinced by our own performances that we didn't see the need to convince anyone else. Except for my grandmother, Oma Schall, a resolute and strict businesswoman. I had to get a positive judgement from her, convince her that I was highly talented, that I had chosen the correct career. An opportunity presented itself when the Municipal Theatre put on a guest performance of Shakespeare's *Twelfth Night* in Stendal, the city where my grandmother had lived since the terrible night of 16 January 1945 when bombs had driven her from her home on Agnetenstraße in Magdeburg. I was playing Sebastian, Viola's brother, as an understudy. Viola's role was much larger than Sebastian's and consequently (according to the way I thought back then) less suited for making a big impression. What to do? Oma Schall was sitting in the front row. In the third scene of Act IV, Sebastian spoke a monologue in Oliva's garden that had been severely truncated by the director, and even so never could have competed with the heartfelt outpourings of Romeo. I stepped onto stage and began:

SEBASTIAN

> This is the air, that is the glorious sun,
> This pearl she gave me, I do feel't and see't,
> And though 'tis wonder that enwraps me thus,
> Yet 'tis not madness. Where's Antonio then?

That was enough information to move the plot of *Twelfth Night* along. Now things could really get going! I shifted to my most pathetic register and let Romeo loose on my grandmother: 'He jests at scars that never felt a wound.' I took it all the way to the bitter end: 'O that I were a glove upon that hand, / That I might touch that cheek!' Of course I meant grandmother's cheek – I had to sweep her off her feet. All that remained was to bring Sebastian's monologue to an end:

> There's something in't
> That is deceivable. But here the lady comes.

I had spoken the cue line perfectly and a slightly confused Olivia could now enter. Afterwards I was reprimanded, but Oma thought it was 'very nice'. I had really hoped for more praise.

Back then, when you applied for an engagement at a theatre you provided a résumé and a list of the fragments that you had worked on. Unfortunately these fragments stood under the rubric 'roles studied' and not 'roles played', a list that was of course much shorter and included few famous or important roles. I auditioned for a few theatre directors at the theatre agent Lieban's offices on Fasanenstraße and was subsequently engaged in Frankfurt an der Oder. Then the following occurred: 'It pleases me to read', wrote the director Willy Linke, 'that you have studied [Don] Carlos, dear Schall' (as long as I live I'll never get used to this 'dear Schall'). 'Luckily I also have an Eboli and a Posa ready to go, and old Richard Milewski has been playing King Philipp for decades, so we can get a production together in fourteen days, no problem. And fourteen days later (I see here that you've also studied Leon) we'll follow it up with Grillparzer's *Thou Shalt Not Lie*. What do you say to that? That's how theatre schedules are made.' Thank God I'm a fast learner. Everything happened as described.

For the major classics, we sometimes got the costumes en bloc from a rental house in Berlin. Then they were tailored to fit, to the extent this was possible. I remember how proud I was when I found the name of a famous Berlin actor, Clemens Hasse, written into the costume I wore for the role of the kitchen-boy Leon. Besides that, in a biography of Joseph Kainz I found a photo of Kainz as Leon in a striking pose: he had his right hand on the nape of his neck, his left hand on his hip and his right foot on a step. He'd turned his head playfully to the left, over his shoulder, and made a generally high-spirited impression. Naturally, I had my picture taken in the same pose and I still have it today.

Things like that made us feel connected to the wide world, which for us, of course, was in the unreachable city of Berlin. We dreamed of gradual advancement in the provinces: of increasingly more important roles in increasingly larger theatres. Our goals were actually fairly modest. Incidentally, *Thou Shalt Not Lie* was the first production in my career that was banned (only later did I remember this and notice the order). The Soviet culture officer banned it personally, directly after the premiere, without explanation. I thought maybe it had to do with Atalus and his barbarians who appear in the play, that he didn't want to see them compared to the Red Army and the Russians. Not that this connection had ever occurred to us. Maybe the title of play also made him uneasy. We had been thrown into cold water and, even though we couldn't swim, we had to paddle if we didn't want to drown.

I was in Frankfurt an der Oder for two years and eight months, until 31 January 1951, and played many roles assigned to me in tragedies, comedies, musical comedies and operettas. Whether I wanted to or not I encountered difficulties, things that didn't make sense when I tried to impose my feelings, my enthusiasm, my personal preferences on them – things needed to be handled differently in order to be performed. I assume that the same thing happens to every gifted and uninhibited young actor. In addition to all this, I began to become conscious of a reality that was not always pleasant. Left to my own devices for the first time, this reality forced and challenged me to pay attention, observe, participate, intervene and accomplish more than ever before. The friction between my own needs and the unavoidable needs of other people, organisations and, indirectly, other nations pushed me into a crisis of acting that lasted for many years. To overcome this crisis I required the help of many people: teachers, directors, personal and political friends – role models, more than anything.

Later, my most important mentor was to be, without a doubt, Bertolt Brecht. But in Frankfurt an der Oder my friends Helga Raumer, Ellen van den Velden and Werner Dissel helped me orientate myself in the city and do justice to both the exciting and the boring roles that I played month by month. These friends took me under their wing and shared their experience with me. They showed me how to give life its fullest quality; they set the bar for acting higher than I was used to, both conceptually and technically. Watching Helga, I learned a naturalness that I didn't have. Ellen shone with a meditative calm that seemed other-worldy, and Werner's multifaceted artistic talent – he could speak, explain, perform, produce, write and paint – caused me to see my own work in a more universal light, to approach it in a more nuanced way. But it was a long path to independence, to artistic autonomy. One kind of awkwardness after another had to be dismantled; one gap in my knowledge after another had to be acknowledged and then filled. Work and conversation brought me further towards these goals and made me more well rounded. I took part in a great many of Brecht's productions and left each one a little more shaken in my abilities. For a while I didn't know how to raise my arm or put my foot down correctly. But these artistic crises, like all of my numerous later ones, were necessary to reach a new level, take on a new quality, to master new techniques and think new thoughts.

Brecht's Epic Theatre of the twenties and early thirties was an ideological and practical polemic against many types of German theatre of the time: naturalism, expressionism, classicism [klassikanisch], theatre of the Bildungsbürgertum, dramatic character-driven theatre and individual-psychological theatre. He wanted to avoid unnecessary emphasis on character qualities or on morality; he wanted to leave the cothurnus and the classical themes (later, also proletarian themes) to heroic or holy figures, he wanted to avoid text that departed from the plot and degenerated into mere recitation. Brecht aimed for a type of performance that he called epic. The main concern of this performance should be to locate the plot of a play, the sum and sequence of all incidents in the play which Aristotle had called 'the first essential, the life and soul, so to speak, of tragedy', push it patiently into the foreground and spread it out for the spectator's observation and inspection – and all this without forgetting that theatre is of necessity entertainment. Brecht emphasises this in:

A Short Organum for the Theatre

65

Everything hangs on the 'story'; it is the heart of the theatrical performance. For it is what happens between people that provides them with all the material that they can discuss, criticise, alter. Even if the particular person represented by the actor has ultimately to fit into more than just the one episode, it is mainly because the episode will be all the more striking if it reaches fulfilment in a particular person. The 'story' is the theatre's great operation, the complete fitting together of all the gestic incidents, embracing the communications and impulses that must now go to make up the audience's entertainment.

German fascism, the Second World War, oppression and genocide in the east and west, new weapons that could destroy all of humanity (and that many times over, so that the high number of 'overkills' was laughably pointless), the hardening of relations between states in two opposing poles of power – these and many other awful things led Brecht to restrict his suggestions about the world and theatre in the world to the most essential aspects. He did away with the term 'Epic Theatre' and introduced the term 'Dialectical Theatre'. He recommended, with his characteristic modesty that always jumped out at me, maybe because he meant it to (Brecht allegedly asked someone once: what is it that you're being so modest about?), that young people read works on materialist dialectics, such as Marx and Engels's *Communist Manifesto*. He advised us not only to concentrate on the short introduction and the first chapter, 'Bourgeois and Proletarians', just because he had restricted himself to these two parts when he adopted it into hexameter near the end of the war, but rather also to read chapters two and three, 'Proletarians and Communists' and 'Socialist and Communist Literature'. He also recommended Lenin's 'On the Question of Dialectics' (which Lenin had written 1914–15 in Swiss exile, after studying Hegel's *Logic* and *History of Philosophy* among other works), and Mao Tse-Tung's essay 'On Contradiction' from August of 1937, which took Lenin's essay as an impetus and developed its ideas further in a Chinese context. Here's an excerpt from that work:

> To consolidate the dictatorship of the proletariat or the people's dictatorship is precisely to prepare the conditions for liquidating such a dictatorship and advancing to the higher stage of abolishing all state systems. To establish and develop the Communist Party is precisely to prepare the condition for abolishing the Communist Party and all party systems. To establish the revolutionary army under the leadership of the Communist Party and to carry on the revolutionary war is precisely to prepare the condition for abolishing war for ever. These contradictory things are at the same time complementary. [Mao Tse-Tung, 'On Contradiction', International Publishers]

In Brecht's 1954 poem 'First Half' is the line:

> I read Voltaire's letters and Mao's essay on contradiction.

In a letter to Yüan Miau-Tse from 31 August 1955 he wrote: 'In the theatre, we've benefited a lot from Mao Tse-Tung's essay "On Contradiction".'

In his answer to a survey by *Neue Deutsche Literatur* in 1954, he named Mao's essay as the best book of the year. After Brecht's death, when open animosity between China and the Soviet Union had broken out, an agent from the cultural ministry forbade me from including one of Brecht's poems, in which he mentions reading Mao's work, in my performance for a party assembly. I protested and ignored the ban in other performances. The People's Republic of China had been declared a *populus non gratus* and Mao a *persona non grata*. That was how Brecht indoctrinated and taught us, and we had fun all the while. Already during the rehearsals of Johannes R. Becher's *Winter Battle* there was a row between Brecht and the actor playing private Johannes Hörder, Knight of the Iron Cross – Schall. This quarrel continued after the premiere of the play and caused Brecht to write a letter to 'The Actor Playing Young Hörder in *Winter Battle*', which he didn't send, but rather let me know in passing that I should pick up a copy of the next *Neue Deutsche Literatur*, because I would read in it a letter pertaining to me:

According to the evening news and your own statements, you still seem to be having considerable difficulties in your portrayal of young Hörder. You complain that on many evenings you don't strike the right tone in one particular scene, which causes everything that follows to go wrong of its own accord. We've occasionally warned you about the term 'strike the right tone', because it implies a particular style of acting which is, in our opinion, not correct. When you say 'the right tone' you don't mean 'natural inflection'. With 'striking the right tone' you seem to mean a procedure like the one that takes place in shooting booths at carnivals, where an entire musical mechanism is set into motion when a shot strikes the bullseye at the centre of a target. We don't mean to be insulting by using this comparison with a carnival – we aim to 'strike' something that is not unworthy, but rather incorrect.

What has happened is that on one hand you haven't fixed the role enough, meaning that the tone can slip away from you, and on the other hand you've fixed it too much, so that the tone struck in one scene makes all the other scenes dependent on it. The expression 'to fix' is also a dubious one. We're using it in a different way, in the way that a drawing can be 'fixed' to be made permanent.

In reality you should not try to fix a particular tone, but rather the stances [*Verhalten*] of the actors on stage, independent from (if also occasionally connected to) the tone of a given scene. And the most important thing is your stance towards your figure, which determines your figure's stance. What do you think about that?

The description that followed dealt in greater detail with the attitudes or stances of individual figures within the play and proved useful. However, Brecht seems to have missed how he was actually promoting the type of 'fixation' that he'd condemned. I had great difficulties more than anything with the monologues in snow and ice, especially the condemned hero's death monologue in the one-man bunker where a live hand grenade will be dropped through the ventilation hole if he does not decide to shoot himself within three minutes. The director of the play helped me very little (on the contrary). When I followed his suggestions, I felt more inhibited and less sure of myself. Becher's undramatic and ungestural texts got on Brecht's nerves, and he demanded of me a listless, mechanical performance: say everything in a monotone as quickly as possible, now without sound, only with air and without stopping, no, without taking a breath, until you can't go on, until you turn blue, then take a quick breath and speak until you can't go on, and so on to the end, don't think about the text, just speak.

The explosion following the monologue, which was supposed to be like Roland's call to Emperor Olifant, made Hörder fall silent. In the end, he died as an anti-fascist, after several terribly long minutes of fear and torment. The decisive change in my approach to the role came one afternoon after rehearsal, when Brecht invited me to his apartment in the Chauseestraße. We sat down and he had me narrate the entire role, the text and my movements, along with what I thought about it, what moved me, and what I imagined while I acted. I spoke about Hörder in the third person, as if talking about some else. This was a simple way of 'episising'

As Johannes Hörder in Johannes R. Becher's Winter Battle, *1955*
(photo by Percy Paukschta)

the part, a technique that can lead to the easy mastery of a role. Brecht and I had another friendly encounter during the rehearsals for the same play, when he taught me respect and love for meter using a Hölderlin quote that Becher had woven into the text. He sat at the small, wobbly harmonium, which stands today in the piano room in Buckow to the right of the window, and accompanied his thin, almost crow-like speech-song [*Sprechgesang*] with two fingers (just as he typed), pressing on the squeaky bellows with his feet:

> Oh, if there were a banner, a Thermophylae
> where I could honourably let it bleed to death
> all the lonely love for which I never find a use!
> [Adapted from Hölderlin, *Hyperion and Selected poems*, ed. Eric Santner]

He valued how the escalation of emotion was supported (and, actually, made possible in the first place) through metrical changes. [In the German original] two lines of normal iambs (a sequence of one short, then one long syllable) are followed by the sudden intrusion at the beginning of the third line of a trochee (one long syllable followed by one short syllable), then followed again and further augmented by a dactyl (one long syllable followed by two shorter syllables), which continued via four hard trochees to one single final stressed foot. During rehearsals for Erwin Strittmatter's play *Katzgraben* he emphasised how important it was to take the verse seriously. He had convinced Strittmatter to take his farmer's comedy in prose and dress it up in classical costume, to outfit the little people with the language of kings. Strittmatter succeeded in this, writing in a nice cottage that used to be the gardener's house, one of a series of row houses on a slope next to Brecht's house in Buckow. Brecht pointed out the useful beauty of metrical language again and again, but he also furiously demanded that the actors honour the enormous extra work that the writer had put into the piece by assimilating the text exactly. The premiere of *Winter Battle* was successful. When I came into my dressing room after the applause, the attendant told me that Brecht had just been there. In my make-up box I found a folded note, smaller than a page from an octavo notebook, upon which was written in barely legible red ink:

Dear Schall,
if I may say so: I find hörder now to be of great quality.
Yours,
b

But he wanted to take the note back after the next evening's performance. He bellowed at me: 'What kind of rubbish was that? What do you think you're doing? Do you think I have time to burn?' Something like that. Thank God I didn't have the note with me that night, or I wouldn't have it today.

What had gone wrong? Earlier in the day I had received a message from Paul Wandel, the Minister of Education. He had been at the premiere the night before and had found the way that Hörder died to be unworthy of an anti-fascist. The seeming cowardice on display in the performance had also disturbed other comrades and former prisoners (although Hörder didn't take the easy way out and shoot himself, he forced the murderers to murder). I took this information with me into the second performance. I didn't intend on playing the role any differently, but I did so in spite of myself. That's how the trouble with Brecht started. When I told Brecht about Wandel's telephone call, how he had purported to speak for others besides himself, Brecht's anger knew no bounds. 'I forbid you from listening to this philistine,' he screamed. 'Just play the part the way we worked out.' I gave it my best effort, but had to struggle with a difficult crisis for the following weeks and months. On top of all this there was a letter, in which I was personally addressed, but which had never been delivered by its addressor. The letter discussed once again the heroism of the main character, which many critics had missed in my performance:

Some critics see the way that Hörder runs away, sobbing like a child while leaving his mother the task of holding his father to account 'pathological'. They probably think that the Prince of Homburg's fear of death is also pathological and, what's worse, they're (almost) all hopeless petty bourgeois who delight in stripping a person of class attributes, in the hopes of uncovering the *real* person, what is universally human about him. The young man is at this moment definitely not a hero and under no circumstances should we speak of heroes 'in their weaker moments, their unheroic moments'. It's much healthier to speak of people in their heroic moments. He [Hörder] doesn't take on the Herculean tasks of Hamlet, nor does he make anything out of his situation. He returns dutifully from his holiday to the front. You're right here, you play this scene completely correctly, with equal parts engagement and superiority, and in doing so you relegate a beloved heroic cliché to the scrap heap of the pantheon of arts, where the masters roam . . .

In the partisan scene, your expression is excellent (though admittedly not to those who scream for heroes): you portray Hörder's contradictory outrage about his refusal to give the command to liquidate the partisans, which is at once a disgust for barbarism and his own insubordination. However, in the death scene, you almost never succeed in finding the mix of the heroic and melancholy tone of a man who has finally come to his senses. In the *War Primer*, which I have never shown you,

Here Brecht's aura of distance, which he cultivated and made no secret about, comes into view

you can see how close you've come to the attitude of the completely confused German soldiers who were met by the Russians near Moscow. [Brecht, GW 16]

A psychological shadow remained with me long after my experience with *Winter Battle*, deepening a crisis that lasted for many months, years even. I examined the notion of the heroic, practically on the stage, and theoretically in writing. In an interview from 7 September 1964 I find the following passage concerning heroism:

> Heroism is a matter of judgement. A hero is a hero because others judge his behaviour in a certain situation to be heroic. Therefore I find heroism to be standpoint-dependent, transferable and teachable (as is the faculty of judgement). I discussed with my colleagues the question: 'What is a hero?' Most of them said that a hero is someone who overcomes his fear or his self-doubt when it matters most. This excludes those who risk their lives to save others without fear or internal struggle. The benefit of heroism is relegated to an internal human attribute. I'm not in favour of making the overcoming of one's fear or self-doubt the main criteria for determining what is heroic, although I admit that conventional heroes are usually forged through danger (or dangerous situations). There is a new point of view, which claims that uncommon industriousness or work under miserable conditions is also heroic. Here, the benefit of heroism is more than an internal human attribute. The new hero and the old hero should be determined historically from the standpoint of social progress, and the discrepancy between internal human attributes and utility should not be too great.

Brecht examined the traces of the past around him carefully, led by a latent caution or fear, which allowed him to track down its relicts and deal with them:

> The One-Armed Man in the Undergrowth
> Dripping with sweat he bends down
> To gather brushwood. The mosquitoes
> He fends off with shakes of the head. Between his knees
> He laboriously bundles his firewood. Groaning
> He straightens himself, holds up his hand to feel
> If it's raining. Hand upraised
> The dreaded S. S. Man.

His interaction with assistants, interns and me (that is, with all of his younger colleagues) was, as I've said before, marked by a feeling of distance that also included mistrust. In his journal entry from 7 July 1954 he noted:

> this country still gives me the creeps. recently when i went out to buckow with young people from the dramaturgs' office, i was sitting in the pavilion while they were working in their rooms or chatting. it suddenly occurred to me that, had i fallen among them ten years ago, all three of them, whatever they had read of mine, would instantly have handed me over to the gestapo . . .

This disdain for the children of Nazis was probably unfair, even if it was partly understandable (when a warrant was issued for the arrest of Carl Friedrich Goerdeler, former mayor of the city of Leipzig, who fled in August of 1944 in the wake of Claus Graf Schenk von Stauffenberg's failed assassination plot, I and all the other *Jungvolk* in Genthin, where we had been sent as a part of the *Kinderlandverschickung*, were rounded up and sent into the streets and forests to catch him). But other things also caused me to notice Brecht's strange way of interacting with me and others. Once I wanted to take a very light but very long kayak out of the old boat shed and carry it two metres to the lake and put it in the water. I was able to lift it easily, but couldn't balance it once I had it off the ground. One end kept tipping downwards. I also couldn't drag it along the ground or it would have broken apart. With two people, the whole thing would have been child's play, the matter of half a minute. Brecht came strolling along with his cane and observed my problem with interest and seriousness. He assured me: there's no way you can balance that boat alone. This afternoon (it was mid-morning) Lindemann (Helene Weigel's chauffeur) is coming from Berlin, and I'll send him to you right away. He'll help you. I had to admit it: Brecht was helpful in spirit.

It wasn't just our generations that differentiated and divided us. Our generations did overlap for many years, but along different paths of development, with no attention to the other on our part. The anti-fascist generation and the generation that I belonged to lived on secretly against one another under the after-effect of our images of the respective enemy. Our childhood indoctrination and an uncompromising approach to life such as Brecht's could not simply be pushed aside, even in times like ours when they no longer functioned (if one can even speak of negative functioning). The same was true of Brecht: he was eager to talk to us and enriched us with his useful friendliness, but his personality remained alien to us. To communicate with or to learn from him meant being ready to admit to ourselves repeatedly that almost everything that we had been, that we had learned or the way in which we had expressed ourselves was morally indefensible and bad, and what's more had to be judged as false (both humanly and historically). On top of this we learned (and this was never articulated, only a general feeling) that we would never be pupils of Brecht, but rather beginners in a new social space, apprentices of an unknown chemistry or alchemy. In order to argue with him, we had to begin from zero, contrite and careful. Today things are very different: today's youth draws on an embarrassment of riches from the past, with confidence, even if it is an utterly wrong (yet victorious) past. We on the other hand couldn't draw on anything but a vacuum, a well that had run dry and was poisoned as well. A beginning and a direction were the most important prerequisites for life. It became clear that a beginning and any one of many inter-changeable directions in life were the most passable roads to old age – except for Brecht and a certain small number of exemplary people whom I met at the crossroads of my youth. Brecht gave, and he took away, that's the truth. Grand plans can't be conveyed pedagogically, you have to muster up the interest (and the right measure of talent), you have to have the necessary gifts and the ability. Back then, Brecht seemed an old man, but at the same time he was much younger than I am today. He felt much the same as I do these days, as evidenced in his journal:

3 nov 52
when i read in a book 'a man of forty-seven', i think, what, he still
wants to be listened to? and i myself am fifty-three.

Today, the divide between the generations in Germany is more
keenly present and more sharply felt than in other places or under
normal circumstances. The Stobber river runs through Buckow,
where I sit by the lake and write. This stream, which drives many
mill wheels, comes in from the red Luch, flows to the Oder, and
the waters beyond the Luch flow to the Havel and the Elbe. The
watershed is not an arbitrary dividing line but a natural one, and is
reliable, as long as humans do not interfere. And the divide
between the generations is reliable as well: mature adults slide into
the ranks of the departing aged. The title of the following elegy
weighs on the rest of the poem like a heavy burden on a donkey,
like a memory burdens an old man:

Difficult Times

Standing at my desk
Through the window I see the elder tree in the garden
And recognise something red in it, something black
And all at once recall the elder
Of my childhood in Augsburg.
For several minutes I debate
Quite seriously whether to go to the table
And pick up my spectacles, in order to see
Those black berries again on their tiny red stalks.

Here, too, curiosity, hesitation and the feeling of having denied
oneself something have great significance. I came to be walled in
by my repertoire many times over, although I still had the wish to
see more of the world, which for me meant meeting other
directors, actors and writers. On 18 May 1953 Hans Henny Jahnn
wrote the following letter to Brecht, care of the German Academy
of Arts:

Dear Brecht!

I've seen your *Señora Carrar's Rifles*. I was very inspired by the performance and profited further from having seen the young actor Ekkehard Schall on stage. I happen to be looking for a young and able actor for my *Spur des dunklen Engels*. In fact, the West Berlin production is entirely dependent on finding such an actor. Admittedly, I don't know if Schall wants to or is allowed to perform in West Berlin. I'm also working on a new piece, *Thomas Chatterton*. The main role would also be played by a young actor.

With warmest regards,

Hans Henny Jahnn

I found out about Brecht's refusal of the offer, along with the offer itself, only in 1996. He had dictated a shorthand note:

Dear Jahnn,

I've informed Ekkehard Schall that the Germans from the east side won't be keeping the appointments you've suggested. . . .

Concerning the splendid piece *Spur des dunklen Engels*: I'd love to help, but how? In principle I'm completely in favour of all actors also performing in West Berlin; it would of course be possible now and then. But young Schall is in almost all of our productions, and I can tell that he is an irreplaceable member of our ensemble, and will have to continue to play his roles with us. That would, of course, greatly hinder preparations for your play. Nevertheless, I suggest that the theatre take up negotiations with us. . . .

Cordially yours,

Jahnn, who didn't give up and offered the Berliner Ensemble *Thomas Chatterton* (the play mentioned in his letter) for performance, received the following refusal this time:

Berlin, 3 June 1955

Dear Jahnn,

Your play is good and does indeed entice me, but I have just as few lead actors for it as I do for half of my own pieces. Schelcher isn't young enough, and Schall hasn't progressed far enough for such a nuanced figure. You can't put on a play about meaningful people without meaningful actors. If there's another war, then we won't be able to put on any more plays at all. – Hopefully I'll see you soon.

cordially

Yours

I learned about these deliberations and appraisals of my ability only after the publication of Brecht's journals. But what's true is true: I was occupied from Monday morning to late in the evening at the weekend; I had over twenty productions and loads of rehearsals. The rehearsal time for plays that Brecht produced himself (like *The Caucasian Chalk Circle*) extended up to a year, including two months of vacation. You had to be present at every rehearsal, which was, admittedly, beneficial, but has meanwhile become a scourge among foolish and tyrannical directors. So, with a deep sigh, I had to turn down Fritz Kortner's offer to perform with him in Munich. I had the opportunity twice, once as Prince Henry in Shakespeare's *Henry IV*, once as the servant Jean in August Strindberg's *Miss Julie*, but it was not meant to be.

Berlin, 25 January 1956

Dear Mr Müller,

Although the prospect of performing under the direction of Herr Kortner quite excites me, it will prove impossible for me to accept your flattering offer for the reasons below:

1. The co-ordinated rehearsals for Brecht's *Galileo* and Synge's *The Playboy of the Western World*, which take up a large part of my time, will certainly last until the end of March, and perhaps into April.

2. I perform in every piece in our repertoire, with a single exception. I am indispensable in only two of these roles; substitutes could be found for the rest of them, though it would be difficult. Were I to take leave from the Ensemble, the performance schedule here would have to be kept intact, which would require me to be

dispensable at an as-yet-to-be-determined date. I bid you farewell with regret and great respect.

I was too busy [*gedrückt und gesülzt*] for a sorrowful refusal. Up until the fall of the wall I was never able to take on theatre work outside the Berliner Ensemble, despite the attractive offers.

At Brecht's rehearsals there was no theorising. If difficulties arose, he marched to the 'Turmzimmer' (tower room) with the entire gang, and they returned only after the dramaturgical error that had been encountered was cleared up. That could last a long time and the actors had to wait. They were excluded from the dramaturgical discussions. Sometimes the rehearsals lasted a long time, days, until the brain gang reappeared in the theatre, led by Brecht, and the interrupted rehearsal continued under new conditions, which were not necessarily explained to us.

From this work process, which created an inner circle, the impression arose outside the theatre that the Berliner Ensemble, collective in general was esoteric and elitist. Naturally some of us, certainly not everyone, but especially those who were closely and strongly identified with the ensemble, were different from the colleagues at other theatres, precisely because the experiment that Brecht and Weigel had started was unique: to reduce the expressivity and co-ordination of a group of actors to the essentials through reason, to change in the direction of the essential. Whereas others sought effects, we abandoned them. We rejected the high demands of individuals in the production and privileged the value of the relationships between the figures. This behaviour absorbed the grand emotions and, where they broke through with violence or real strength, they were not spared the behaviour of others. To the extent that we took Brecht seriously, we underwent some painful farewells and were not always immediately praised individually. But when we received individual praise it was remarkable. In many cities around the world we felt respected, less so in Germany.

In the magazine *Konkret. Politik und Kultur*, Vol. 10, 1997, Jan Knopf writes:

In 1954, after the Berliner Ensemble's guest performance of Mother Courage in Paris, the 'révolution brechtienne' broke out in France, fuelled by Roland Barthes's euphoric lead article in *Théâtre Populaire* on the new 'Epic Theatre'. Brecht's worldwide success could no longer be denied, and the West German intellectuals worked themselves to the bone trying to qualify all the political aspects of Brecht's works as superficial, and to reduce his work to the 'essence' of literature (by the way, these attempts were sometimes quite successful and revealed new, sometimes decidedly strange, dimensions in his work).

From the editorial in *Théâtre Populaire* II, 1955, page 1:

Aristotelian theatre has been performed in Europe for more than 2,400 years. Whenever we go to the theatre, whether to see something by Shakespeare or Montherlant, by Racine or by Roussin, to see Maria Casarès or Pierre Fresnay, we judge what we find pleasing or disappointing, good or evil, valuable and tenable – even today in 1955 – based on a morality that is centuries old. This morality's credo is: the more awestruck the audience, the stronger its identification with the hero, the more faithful the representation of events on the stage, the more intense the actor's embodiment of his role, the more magical the theatre, the better the performance. And all at once a man comes along whose work and ideas question the basis of this type of art, which has been regarded as 'natural' as if handed down from the most ancient times. This man tells us, against all tradition, that the spectator should involve himself only half-heartedly with the play, he should only 'experience' what happens, not suffer along with it. In order to bring about this attitude in the audience, the actor should not embody his role, rather put it on display. The spectator should not ceaselessly identify with the hero, rather preserve his ability to judge the causes of the hero's suffering and how he may be helped. Events should not be acted out, rather reported. Theatre should no longer be magical, rather critical and, in being so, has the best chance of touching people's hearts, says this man.

Because Brecht's theatrical revolution questions our inclinations, reflexes, habits, in fact, the 'laws' of theatre in general, we can no longer remain silent or take an ironic stance, we must confront Brecht . . .

Mother Courage
by Bertolt Brecht
A performance by the Berliner Ensemble at the *Théâtre Sarah Bernhardt* reviewed by Roland Barthes in Théâtre *Populaire*

This dramaturgy, with its revolutionary ideas, is the only one fit to justify theatre itself today. We should admit to being shaken by the *Mother Courage* of the Berliner Ensemble: like every great work, Brecht's work is a critique of a previous evil. *Mother Courage instructs* us. The performance gives us material for years of contemplation, and a rare pleasure as well: the experience of how a fundamental critique can be combined with the ideals we postulate about liberated theatre in its most mature and complete form.

On 14 October 1954 Heinz Hofmann wrote about the 7 October German premiere of *The Caucasian Chalk Circle* in the East Berlin *National-Zeitung* [*National Newspaper*], in an article entitled 'Brecht against Brecht in the "Caucasian Chalk Circle"':

Brecht, who has always clearly favoured a form appropriate to content, and who spends an above-average amount of time experimenting before each production, hasn't arrived at his own unified form in the *Chalk Circle*, but, by persisting in ideas thoroughly in need of revision, has come in turn to disconcerting and confusing solutions. These solutions threaten to pitch our theatrical workers into inner chaos and doubt during a time when Germany is divided, a time when we require a conscious reflection on our national experience and on Stanislavsky's valuable proposals . . .

Therefore we must differentiate between the *work* and its *performance* because Brecht the director has turned in subjective goodwill objectively against Brecht the writer . . . The invalid's mask appears gruesome and therefore against all theatrical aesthetics. The bottle of embrocation for the amputee is open mockery. It would behove the production to strike this scene entirely, because it pushes the limits of the humanistic considerably.

This was not a reckoning between the central committee of the SED [Socialist Unity Party of Germany] and the annoyance named Brecht. The central committee took absolutely no notice of the *Chalk Circle* production. This was a single querulous voice (that is, in this case, a writer from the NDPD, the German National Democratic Party, one of the block of parties which was represented in the GDR as the German Democratic National Front). In the professional journal *Theater der Zeit*, Vol. 12, 1954, Fritz Erpenbeck, the leader of the phalanx against Brecht, wrote two articles: one entitled 'Epic Theatre or Dramatic Art?', the other, a critical appraisal, entitled 'The Caucasian Chalk Circle'. A few excerpts follow:

This concerns the German author Bertolt Brecht, who wrote and produced *The Caucasian Chalk Circle*, the German author, whose work is known throughout the cultural world. It concerns the German author Bertolt Brecht who finds a very specific path in theatrical art and acting to be worth taking, the author whose towering artistic personality as a practical man of the theatre seems exemplary. The question is merely whether you approve or disapprove of his aesthetics, if you think that his creative path is the path to the future of German theatre. If it is such a path, then we must conclude, that dramatists, directors and actors, especially the young ones, should study the 'Organum' diligently, and make lively and sensible use of it in their own Epic Theatre, to the extent that it appeals to their inclinations and talents.

But if you think, as the writer of these lines does, that this path is fundamentally wrong, then candour demands of us to warn with concern: Caution, dead end!

How simply the matter presents itself . . .

Since 1945, I've often described and justified my standpoint concerning not only Brecht's work, but also contemporary American and Soviet stage productions. I refuse to see Epic Theatre as an acceptable path into the future . . .

There is no such thing as epic *drama*, because (and no one contests this fact) drama means to act, not to narrate. Were this not true, we'd have to also speak of 'dramatic drama' (as a contrast) in the future . . .

One can't avoid the simple choice: for or against Epic Theatre . . .

The Berliner Ensemble's next guest performance in Paris (this time it was the *Chalk Circle*) at the Sarah Bernhardt Theatre from 20 to 24 July 1955, brought us a further triumph after the accolades of the previous year. Those stubborn fighters who campaigned against Brecht and for Konstantin Stanislavsky (a great man of the theatre who couldn't do anything about the way he was being used) continued to write embittered articles, but lost their significance with time.

In the Federal Republic of Germany, on the other hand, a boycott of Brecht's work began to spread, making it harder to perform his works there. In the Bundestag, Heinrich von Brentano, Foreign Minister of the Federal Republic of Germany (1955–61), defamed Brecht (who had recently died) with a remark that aimed below the belt. It was in extraordinarily poor taste, and could only be explained by blind hatred.

Berliner Zeitung, Berlin, 10 May 1957

Brentano equates Brecht with Horst Wessel

Bonn. During budget discussions for the Bonn Ministry of Foreign Affairs in the Bundestag, the SPD [German Social Democratic Party] delegate Kahn-Ackermann sharply criticised the Ministry's cultural politics. He condemned the delay in the processing of visas for three Soviet actors, and further criticised the cancellation of grants to the Bochum Theatre, which wanted to perform pieces by Bertolt Brecht in Paris. Foreign Minister Brentano replied that the selection of Brecht's work for the guest performance in Paris 'couldn't justify support from the scant means of the Foreign Ministry'. Finally, he made the outrageous remark that Bert Brecht's poetry could only be compared to Horst Wessel's.

This propagandistic statement, which was not contradicted by any other government official, ushered in a new type of interaction with representatives of the other German state, the GDR, which forbade itself such remarks.

There is no correspondence between national socialist and communist thought. The analytic followers of communism pointed out a deficiency, a seed of destruction that the capitalist system carries within itself. Their intentions were to help actively those neglected by the public welfare: the proletariat. In contrast, fascist and national socialist thinkers speak of a population surplus, which must be corrected through the decimation of the superfluous population. The 'Malthusian Law' of population growth moved many minds in a serious and inhumane way. Thomas Robert Malthus (1766–1834) wrote an 'Essay on the Principle of Population'. Since I couldn't find a German copy of his work, I'll quote from Wahrig's *Wörterbuch* and Meyer's *Konversationlexikon* from 1897. Malthus believed that:

the world would perish of hunger because the earth's population was expanding more rapidly than its potential for agricultural production, and therefore recommended drastic measures to stem population growth (war, contraception, etc.) . . .

[Malthus believed that] populations have the tendency to reproduce more quickly than the means of nourishment they require . . .

Various checks stand in the way of the population's natural reproductive drive . . . either preventative, that is, those that prevent the development of a large population . . . or repressive, those that reduce already existing populations (emigration, war, scarcity, misery, illness, abortion, infanticide, child abandonment). Repressive checks are felt first and foremost in the weaker elements of society, especially among the children of the poor, whose mortality rate is raised due to a lack of nutrition and care. [Malthus] denounces a population policy aiming for population growth as useless and detrimental, because its backward measures (misguided care for the poor) can easily lead to the development of a dependent, sickly population (proletariat).

At its heart, Malthusianism was Nazi thought and lives on today in different forms, such as the inequality of opportunity which determines the policy of many national and international capitalist enterprises and which also determined the policy of the absorption of the GDR into the FRG, a move which many felt to be a colonial gesture and was called as much. Marx countered Malthus's law of population with the statement that it gave 'expression to capital's brutal views' [*Philosophisches Wörterbuch*, eds Georg Klaus and Manfred Buhr].

Karl Marx and Friedrich Engels laid down the principles of their philosophy in the *Communist Manifesto*:

I

Bourgeois and Proletarians . . .

In the conditions of the proletariat, those of old society at large are already virtually swamped. The proletarian is without property; his relation to his wife and children has no longer anything in common with the bourgeois family relations; modern industrial labour, modern subjection to capital . . . has stripped him of every trace of national character. Law, morality, religion are to him so many bourgeois prejudices, behind which lurk in ambush just as many bourgeois interests.

And further:

II

Proletarians and Communists

The theoretical conclusions of the communists . . . merely express, in general terms, actual relations springing from an existing class struggle, from a historical movement going on under our very eyes. . . . The distinguishing feature of communism is not the abolition of property generally, but the abolition of bourgeois property. . . . But modern bourgeois private property is the final and most complete expression of the system of producing and appropriating products, that is based on class antagonisms, on the exploitation of the many by the few.

For what use would dialectic be, were it not useful or employable? A contradiction in society can be sublated, even in an artistic, fictional sense, only when you pit the viewpoint of the most wronged against the viewpoint of the most powerful, simply put, poverty against riches, powerlessness against power, vulnerability against violence. When confronting thought that has existed for centuries you also have to underscore and defend new insight against ossified opinion, goodness of heart against cold condemnation. The love for humanity needs reason much more than the law of the well-to-do, but the well-to-do have loaned out reason for their own purposes and perverted it into irrationality.

Let me return to Brentano's Brecht–Wessel constellation, which was a coupling of opposites: Brecht, the genius whose writings championed reason, who searched for evidence to back his opinions all his life, and Wessel, who revelled in street violence with his *Sturmabteilung* and had no need of evidence. Brecht had been compared to (or, to put it better, equated to) a Nazi and now popular socialism (not only socialism's Stalinist perversion) could be compared and equated with Nazism. Brecht's attempt (which proved unpopular in socialist countries) to show the socialist community to be intellectually superior, at least on the stage, had now been rejected, sometimes even demonised, in both the West and the East. It was a grand coalition of sorts, two warring factions allied against Brecht. The communists in the government didn't realise how much power they lost by not laying claim to Brecht in the way he would have liked; they didn't notice how they helped to prepare capitalism's victory when they shoved people like Brecht aside without a second thought, without accepting his help.

Although it was not apparent to all those involved, the new widespread attack on Brecht was a sort of secret back-room dealing at the expense of the progressive spirit. I see Brentano and his clever cronies in front of me, rubbing their hands in glee at their coup that had succeeded in defaming Brecht, in debasing Brecht the left-winger with this Nazi. Now they could drag socialism through the muck with impunity.

Sonntag Berlin, 26 May 1957
The Berliner Ensemble Protests
    A delegation of the Berliner Ensemble, currently in Moscow,

including among others Ernst Busch, Angelika Hurwicz, Wolf von Beneckendorff, Regine Lutz, Wolf Kaiser, Martin Flörchinger, Erich Franz and me

> went last Saturday to the West German embassy in the Soviet capital to deliver a letter of protest. The spokesperson for the Ensemble was also its oldest artist, Wolf von Beneckendorff, a great-nephew of Paul von Hindenburg. Despite being present the West German ambassador refused to receive the artists.

In the letter it says:

> We have read Mr Brentano's statement concerning the great German author who founded and led our theatre until his death, the author whose poetic and dramatic works have brought him immortal fame in all countries of culture, from the Soviet Union to America. We have, ourselves, witnessed ten thousand spectators professing enthusiastic agreement with Bertolt Brecht's work, in Vienna and Warsaw, in Paris and London, in our homeland in Berlin and Munich, and now in Moscow . . . This fills us with honour and pride, because on our journeys we have learned that Brecht belongs to those Germans who win back the respect and trust of other nations for our fatherland, the trust that Mr Brentano and like-minded others had gambled away so bloodily . . . We stand proudly with Brecht, whom your Foreign Minister has defamed.

With this defamation he has attempted to finish the work that his predecessor, the book burner Hitler, had begun. Our knowledge of historical development tells us that this attempt will end no better for Mr Brentano, lover of SA poetry, than it did for those pyre builders and their crony Horst Wessel, now registered as a 'German Poet' in Bonn. May our people be spared from once again footing the bill for such aesthetic taste. We, Brecht's colleagues and students, assure you and your Foreign Minister that we will do everything it takes to prevent this from happening.

Brecht was a red flag for the petty bourgeois and petty bourgeois critics of every stripe. They built a united front in the GDR, FDR and the Republic of Austria, employing weapons of malice, hatred, boycott, lies and slander to ensure that his theatre would be moved to the back burner of cultural life and remain there.

This didn't end after Brecht's death. The animosity was adapted to Weigel and us, her young team. At times the FRG fought us like the plague. Our incompetence and errors, our attitude as well, were piled on top of (or multiplied by) all of the attitudes and errors attributed to Brecht.

Extra

Scandal in Frankfurt

The Bert Brecht-Ensemble is a Pankow Functionary Corps

WHILE PANKOW DIVIDES BERLIN, EAST BERLINER CULTURAL FUNCTIONARIES PERFORM IN THE FRANKFURTER SCHAUSPIELHAUS!

This scandalous development led the CDU [Christian Democratic Union] faction in the city parliament to deliver the following letter to the mayor.

Honoured Mr Mayor,

Last Monday, CDU members of the city parliament proposed rescinding the invitation to the Bert Brecht-Ensemble from the Schiffbauerdamm Theatre in East Berlin for the guest performance on 14 September 1960 in Frankfurt am Main . . . We wholeheartedly approve of the idea that one should counter Pankow's intolerance with the tolerance of the West. However, this tolerance is misplaced when applied to functionaries of the Pankow rulers, and the Bert Brecht-Ensemble is a corps of Pankow functionaries. The ensemble was dispatched to Frankfurt not to facilitate cultural exchange, but rather to fulfil a political mission, just like the rulers of the Third Reich sent Werner Kraus to Paris to prove to the French that they would only espouse pure art.

When will we finally learn from history! . . .

There it was again, the Nazi comparison – it was coming easier to them with time.

WE ARE SURE THAT IF THE POPULATION OF BERLIN AND THE SOVIET-OCCUPIED ZONES HAD A SAY IN THIS QUESTION, THEY WOULD CONDEMN THE GUEST PERFORMANCE.

In the name of the faction, I remain, with great respect,
signed Ludwig Jost
Head of the CDU faction

FELLOW CITIZENS!
WE FIND OURSELVES IN A BITTER STRUGGLE FOR THE PRESERVATION AND RECLAMATION OF FREEDOM FOR ALL GERMANS. WE WILL LOSE THIS STRUGGLE, AND OUR WELFARE, AND OUR RECONSTRUCTION EFFORTS IN FRANKFURT WILL BE ENDANGERED, IF THIS DANGEROUS SOFTENING PROCESS IS PROMOTED. WHAT GOOD ARE OUR EFFORTS, 'IF THE COSSACKS COME'.

(Johann Friedrich Naumann)

It was a sold-out performance of *Ui*, which took place before an enthusiastic audience. What has come to disgust me the most are those people who, after the rigorous struggles against Brecht in the early years, developed into scholarly parasites who spent (and still spend) their lives exhuming Brecht's corpse. They draw attention to the (often unimportant) results of their dissection, but mainly just to themselves. Where don't you feel 'the foetid breath of provincialism' (from Brecht's journal) that disgusted Brecht in the Rotes Rathaus [Berlin's city hall], where he met with Mayor Friedrich Ebert on 6 January 1949: in the government and in city theatres, in conversations and articles. After every handshake you should wash your hands, after every quotidian reading you should read a little of a classic.

We who dealt with Brecht in the Berliner Ensemble were not what people saw in us, were not what people wished us to be. We were not an order with initiation rites and certainly not the 'Red Monastery' that Brigitte Klump and the college of journalism at the Karl-Marx-University in Leipzig thought us. (Klump, who had worked with us for a time as a dramaturg, authored a book called *Das rote Kloster* [The Red Monastery].) We were a quarrelling bunch of tightly knit, headstrong people. Admittedly, those strong ties were only provisionally present after Brecht's death and finally dissolved completely. Members of the Ensemble became elitist, because they isolated themselves. Even so, they were unable to rid themselves of the stigma of having studied with Brecht. Where are the others? Regine Lutz and Benno Besson are in Switzerland, Carl Maria Weber is in the USA, Fred Düren and Igael Tumarkin are in Israel, Wolfgang Pintzka is in Norway. Scattered around Germany are Uta Birnbaum, Angelika Hurwicz, Käthe Reichel, Vera Skupin, Lothar Bellag, Erwin Geschonneck, Claus Hubalek, Klaus Küchenmeister, Egon Monk, Peter Palitzsch, Hartmut Reck, Heinz Schubert, Peter Voigt, Manfred Wekwerth and others. All these people have little or nothing in common.

Sometimes Brecht interrupted rehearsal because the structure of a scene seemed impossibly written. Who wrote such a thing? he would wonder aloud, agitated. This seemed like hypocrisy to me since he himself was the author. But looking back on it, it was probably a state of secondary (fabricated) naivety that producing his own work brought about in him. 'Secondary naivety' – that's a dialectic that pits itself against itself as an object against an untouched subject.

Brecht was a physical director; he enjoyed demonstration. After much effort to drive the heroism out of Busch's Galileo, to take the edge off the figure despite Busch's resistance, Brecht and Busch (both seasoned veterans) got bogged down in the scene where Galileo, pestered by his student, sits back in an armchair to hold his grand reckoning with the world of science. From repetition to repetition, Busch sat ever more spryly, the tension in his body and his glittering eyes betraying his excitement at the coming reckoning. Brecht, whose stage directions began 'professorially, folding his hands over his stomach', requested that Busch sit down as if old, fragile and half-blind, so that he could then begin speaking with a certain smugness. Busch's incomprehension and intractability seemed to prevent this. So Brecht employed his most powerful weapon: demonstration. He walked from the front of the stage towards the chair, slowly, careful like an old man and feeling about as if blind, and stood calmly after finally arriving in front of the chair. He bent forward a bit until his hands came to rest on the chair's wooden arms, then shifted his weight to both arms equally. He paused again for a moment, so that he could begin to rotate his left shoulder upwards to the right until the critical point had been reached: the left hand had to make a fairly quick jerk to meet the right hand on the other arm of the chair. This move successful, he continued twisting, this time opening his right shoulder backwards, again with a certain quickness, until his right hand gripped the right arm of the chair. This accomplished, he rested both hands on his slightly upward-pointing chest and collapsed into himself. After this short, intentional fall, he sat in the chair, satisfied and exhausted, but with the knowledge that he had mastered the situation cleverly and was still superior to that old Adam he carried inside him. Brecht had found an enthusiastic audience in me: he was my kind of director. Busch continued to play his cantankerous hero.

Then there was [Erwin] Geschonneck's walk to his execution as the Governor in the *Chalk Circle*: led at the end of a rope by the executioner at a markedly slow pace and described by a singer, he

walked over a narrow, long red carpet that traced the radius of a
half-circle. We worked for weeks on the slow-motion portrayal of
incomprehension, of a distortedly long approach to death. Here
Brecht even allowed the action to be doubled with text, which he
usually hated like the devil:

> Just look about you once more, you blind man!
> *The arrested* GOVERNOR *looks about him.*

During one performance, a lighting technician dropped his glasses
on to the stage at exactly this moment.

> Does all that you once possessed still please you? Between the
> Easter Mass and the banquet
> You are walking to that place from which no one returns.
> *The* GOVERNOR *is led away.*

What a staggering end for a ruler, for whom ruling was natural.
What subtle artistry, what content-appropriate aesthetics, playful
scrutiny of the passage of time, long before Robert Wilson.

As the adjunct to the Governor's Wife in the *Chalk Circle*, I
played a proud, energetic, combative young man who made
himself conspicuous through his quick, hard steps like those of a
macho flamenco dancer, standing bolt upright with chin raised like
a Russian soldier on parade. I remember one of the walks Weigel
took as the Governor's Wife, from one proscenium arch towards
me, who stood stiff as a board in front of another arch. She
approached me slowly, steadily and sensually, supported by her
characteristic slightly deepened alto. She said something in a way
that made it clear that we were lovers. Brecht called this gait 'the
million-dollar walk' and it often got my blood pumping. When the
palace revolution broke out, I stormed into the gate at one end of
the above-mentioned red carpet and appeared later at the same
gate facing backwards, striking about myself wildly with my sword
and shouting orders. Brecht recommended that I not let my figure
fall apart during the fighting, rather that I run backwards with the
staccato steps of a sewing machine, swinging my blade rigidly in

front of me, rounding the arc of the carpet and then disappearing. He said I wouldn't need opponents to do this.

I was astonished by this suggestion, and was thinking it over, when Brecht suddenly demonstrated it. Seldom in my life have I seen something happen so quickly: he leapt into the palace gate and scurried immediately back out, sprinting backwards, his back held tense as a toreador's. He sliced through the air with his arms, which seemed to have nothing at all to do with his body. Quick as a jackrabbit, he scuttled round the curved path of carpet with the tiniest steps I had ever seen. My mouth hung open in astonishment. On the one hand it was terribly funny, absurd, silly. On the other hand it ripped the scene wide open, exposing new situational constellations. I took on his suggestion (actually, his assignment) and perfected the backwards run until it had the quality of a film clip run in reverse. But then Kurt Palm, director of the Staatliche Werkstätten [State Studios], gave me a costume made of heavy stiff material and an ankle-length coat with a metre-long train in the back. Brecht held this small man from the Behrenstraße in such high regard that I was forced to come up with something different for my adjunct figure. Brecht's idea, which had been as good as one of his better poems, and all the drudgery I'd put myself through had been for nothing.

Brecht was a woman's director, in the same way as he was a woman's dramatist as a writer. Brecht had written parts for the three mothers, Teresa Carrar, Pelagea Vlassova and Anna Fierling (known as Mother Courage), for Joan Dark, lieutenant of the Black Straw Hats, known as Saint Joan of the Stockyards, Shen Teh, known as the Good Person of Sezuan (along with the pants role Shui Ta), Turandot, the daughter of the Chinese emperor, Simone Machard (in the dream sequences, the virgin of Orleans) and Antigone, daughter of Oedipus. And then there's Polly Peachum and Low-Dive Jenny. Who can sing her songs and not think about her love for Macheath, aka Mack the Knife? And the kitchen maid Grusha Vachnadze, that loyal soul! And Kattrin, the mute daughter of Mother Courage and saviour of the city of Halle!

Brecht valued women as actors and directed them remarkably well.

THE SINGER

After her escape from the Ironshirts
After twenty-two days of wandering
At the foot of the Janga-Tau glacier
From this moment Grusha Vachnadze decided to be the child's mother.

THE SINGER

When Grusha Vachnadze, pursued by the Ironshirts
Came to the narrow footbridge of the Eastern slope
She sang the song of the rotten bridge
And risked two lives.

Once Angelika Hurwicz practised how she would cross the shaky bridge stretched over an imaginary abyss 2,000 feet deep, with a child doll in hand. After Brecht showed her how he meant her to do it, the child seemed even more precious than before. Her steps seemed lighter, more delicate, almost ballet-like, avoiding even the slightest vibration. The hazard and its overcoming were represented without great technical effort and it should have been obvious to the spectators that the solution was a happy one. Like other good directors, Brecht tended to make his performances too long. He couldn't bear to part with any scene once it was finished. But it wasn't any use: any more than three and a half hours with intermission was too much for the bottoms, bladders and attention span of the audience – not to mention the public transport, which didn't run late enough. Cuts had to be made. Many critics also found fault with the long-windedness of the production and, after the premiere, lots of scenes were cut, including the one described above. To those of us involved, this seemed like a painful reverse-birth, the child going from the outside back in.

My first time working with Brecht (during the rehearsals for *Señora Carrar's Rifles*) was a great experience. After her husband is shot while fighting on the front against Franco, a woman vows to protect her sons, come what may, to stay quiet as a mouse and refuse to take part in the battle that can be heard raging nearby.

However, she does not refuse her many visitors the opportunity to agitate for the Republic and the Popular Front, or is unable to prevent it. Withdrawn and reluctant, she takes in what the visitors tell her: the wounded militiaman, Manuela (her son Juan's girlfriend), the cautious Padre, the elderly Señora Perez (her neighbour) and Pedro Jaquéras, the worker who is also her brother. During the rehearsals we showed Carrar's resolve slowly soften with each visitor, her acquiescence gradually develop. She showed pity, expressed reverence for the courage of the population and became uncontrollably furious when she was accused of not taking part in the struggle – all without actually participating in the struggle. Brecht and Weigel (as Carrar) rehearsed the figure of Carrar in this way for weeks, becoming less and less satisfied all the while. The nascent figure didn't properly prepare the inevitable deep fall, when Carrar takes her guns from their hiding place and joins the battle alongside her younger son José, after the corpse of her other son Juan is laid at her feet, riddled with the bullets of Franco's men. She had believed Juan to be in the safe place that she had devised, fishing on the cape. She had thought that no one would be able to influence him or invade his isolation. Her fall could not be far enough. For that reason Weigel's suggestion to make Carrar's resolve gradually harder, not softer, was not unexpected. She made a theatrical about-face. Her body stiffened, her expression became hostile, she held herself like an iron rod instead of a reed. Nothing could change her mind. Any attempt to sway her only strengthened her intractable intention of not resisting Franco, for which there was no cure. This approach proved to be successful: the change was dramatic as her murdered son lay before her; now she would confront his murderers. Carrar had taken on a new and fitting quality.

Weigel, who showed Carrar's stiffness with visible effort during the rehearsals, made things easier on herself during the per-

formances by wearing a stiff, tight corset. You could see the
success of a dialectical mode of performance in the rehearsal
process: the build-up of one negation which, under pressure,
negates itself, or to put it another way, leads to a second negation
of its own first negation.

During my last rehearsal with Brecht on *Life of Galileo* (I played
Andrea, a pupil of Galileo's and son of Frau Sarti) we also had our
last disagreement. It was the final scene: Galileo's former pupil
comes to voice his contempt for his traitorous teacher, who has
been banished to a country home near Florence. The idol of
Andrea's student years has submitted to the authority of the
church, and through this betrayal has ended all progress (and
publication) in the field of astronomy, against his own better
judgement. I played the part with an icy manner, wishing only to
wound my former teacher and escape quickly. This displeased
Brecht, who said something to the effect of: of course you can also
play that scene that way, if you want to be solemn, a man whose
character has become cold, who is not to be touched by the words
of his interlocutor (that is, until the great plot twist when Galileo
hands over the *Discorsi: Discourses Concerning Two New Sciences:
Mechanics and Local Motion* to his student). Andrea has come to
show his contempt for Galileo to be sure, but he has come
nonetheless. If you don't also show the boundlessly injured love
that Andrea has for Galileo, you won't accurately reflect his
disposition. He just wants his old teacher back and nothing more.
And Andrea gets what he wants in spite of Galileo's self-
condemnation and his harsh avowal of the disgrace that could (or
will) befall humanity because of his actions.

The word 'solemn' really struck a nerve with me. I had not
succeeded in delivering a convincing performance with my premeditated iciness. Brecht apparently found it astounding that
anyone (especially me, probably) would want to sustain one stance
(as the epitome of a figure) just to heighten the effect of the plot
twist when Andrea misunderstands his teacher for the last time. I
was following the technique that I had believed I had learned

during the Carrar rehearsals. Change your stance as reactions dictate, Brecht admonished me. Play a contradictory figure all the way through, not just at the crucial moments. Brecht led the rehearsals for *Life of Galileo* from 13 December 1955 until 27 May 1956, when he excused himself due to the illness that would lead to his death.

Erich Engel was first the interim director, then took over as main director. He premiered the production on 15 January 1957. Conflicts of a very different nature from those I had with Brecht arose between Engel and me from the beginning, when we still thought that Brecht would return. Engel wanted to assert himself and wasn't interested in arguing with me; he even changed things that Brecht had already orchestrated. Since we also didn't get along personally, there were some unpleasant scenes between us. He didn't like my acting style at all. He ended our collaboration for ever (which never really got started in the first place) with the line: 'I've been over your expressionism since 1920.' When I substituted for Fred Düren as Andrea (I played the part often) at the Berliner Ensemble's guest performance in Hamburg led by Gustav Gründgens, Engel let me know that he wouldn't sign off on my performance. Trivial matters. Brecht was dead, but I lived on under his influence. I have a whole bagful of memories from my time with him, but I can only scatter a handful of them from time to time about me like chicken feed.

Remarks

Concerning Seriousness
I don't value irony (including sarcasm), not in interaction with other people and above all not in my profession. If irony isn't already a part of a figure's stance, an actor should be cautious in using it. It ruins the believability of an action. An actor's arrogant attitude (whether directed against a standard, a play or opinions contained in the play) doesn't allow for a competent critique to be

formed and is unbearable for someone with aesthetic taste. Plot or story cannot be conveyed through irony. If you're itching to spice things up a bit, then try cynicism instead. At least it dispenses with every element except for hatred.

An actor's thought is thought that is expressed. All other thought is part of the preparation for the role.

I've always been of the opinion that an actor should memorise his role and get acquainted with the play before rehearsals begin. This is to ensure that he is armed with the same weapons as the director who, in today's theatre, often (stupidly) styles himself as the boss.

If something doesn't make sense to you, don't swallow it or choke it down. Present it publicly to the rest of the cast and work it out in discussion.

A systematic approach can help in complicated cases. Systematic training and its effects can be sustained longer.

It is not only gestures that can be comparative; texts can be as well. Both have ascertainable (and quotable) beginnings and ends. I saw a film with Vanessa Redgrave directed by John Irvin titled *A Month by the Lake*. In the beginning the man makes fun of the woman, saying 'your ears are red because you're excited', and the circle of love is closed at the end with the same line, this time from her to him. Not an incredible film, but nevertheless one that has some distinctive elements of theatre acting that appeal to me.

Disagreement, or the spirit of disagreement (which starts in child-hood) is often demoted to stubbornness or 'intransigence', and discredited and mocked. It can start with 'Mother doesn't want me to go out to play' and lead to 'Mother doesn't want me to go to war'. The mother's objectivity can oppose the child's subjective behaviour to a certain extent, within the unity of the mother–child relationship. At first the mother has the upper hand, until an external objectivity supports and renders the son's argument superior. Subjective and objective stances change, those who hold them become interchangeable, but they will always be dependent on and influence each other.

Brecht left many forms of enrichment behind. There was one sentence that concerned me personally in Guy Leclerc's review in *L'Humanité* of the Berliner Ensemble's guest performance of *Mother Courage* from 28 June to 5 July 1954 in Paris. It read: 'I'm thinking of . . . Ekkehard Schall, the "blond angel" of war.' It sounds even better in French: '*L'ange blonde de la guerre.*' I didn't view this as flattery. I enjoyed these words, just as I enjoy the words of Else Lasker-Schüler in her poem '*Prayer*':

> Everywhere I seek a city
> With an angel at its gate
> [Else Lasker-Schüler, *Gesammelte Werke*, Band I]

I had been accorded a poetic honour and, besides that, Brecht's letter from May 1954 had finally borne fruit (see page 33).

With these scattered remarks out of the way, let's return to the crux of our discussion: Brecht's pedagogical opinions, which he disseminated in the form of suggestions made more concrete with technical terms. He wanted us to learn that materialist dialectics were not an invention, but were present as a driving force in living developments. When it came to the theatre, we were meant to assume that his suggestions aimed at raising our dramatic art to the complicated level of real relations by means of dialectic thought. I never heard him make a suggestion twice or check up on someone to make sure that his suggestion had been implemented. What kind of suggestions did Brecht make for the theatre? Let's stick with terms that he introduced, like *Gestus* for example, which means human stance or attitude [*Haltung*], or, to put it better, human behaviour (a component of the dialectic unity comprising behaviour and plot or the unity comprising behaviour and text). Or take, for example, the *Verfremdungseffekt*, which can cause you to become conscious of something that you had forgotten about (it makes contradiction visible, in certain

As Eilif in Brecht's Mother Courage, *1954 (photo by Hainer Hill)*

circumstances even experienceable). Here's Brecht's definition from *The Messingkauf Dialogues*:

> We now come to one of those elements that are peculiar to the epic theatre, the so-called *V-effekt (Verfremdungseffekt)*. What is involved here is, briefly, a technique of taking the human social incidents to be portrayed and labelling them as something striking, something that calls for explanation, is not to be taken for granted, not just natural. The object of the 'effect' is to allow the spectator to criticise from a social point of view. [Translation altered]

With that, much has been said, but little accomplished. What's the big deal here? The new reason for the *Verfremdungseffekt*? The *Verfremdungseffekt* had existed for a long time; Brecht did not invent it. It was a trick intended to surprise, amuse or frighten people. In the film version of *Puntila*, Curt Bois, an excellent comic actor, played the titular role. If I remember correctly, in one scene he came into a chemist's and vigourously shook a skeleton's hand as he passed the place where it stood near the wall. He then turned towards the chemist and started walking in his direction when something seemed strange to him in retrospect. He turned round cautiously and got quite a scare when he recognised the skeleton. [Demonstrated during the seminar.]

This was just a gag, a double take, a delayed effect, but it had the structure of a *Verfremdungseffekt*: habit had played a trick on Puntila.

Then there's Marilyn Monroe. She played a severely near-sighted girl in *How to Marry a Millionaire*. She wants to go into another room to impress a young man there. Of course, she leaves her glasses behind, because she thinks she looks prettier without them. So she sets off smartly and smacks into the wall near the doorway. The *Verfremdungseffekt* in this scene consists of the way that Monroe doesn't show any signs of pain, but acts like the collision is a matter of course, accepts it, merely corrects her direction and proceeds into the neighbouring room, a dazzling smile on her face. She is off to conquer the young man's heart and will probably run into something else again soon enough. [Demonstrated during the seminar.] This gag delivers the near-sighted young woman into the hands of the audience: from now on they will anticipate and expect her to smack into walls.

Immanuel Kant described the *Verfremdungseffekt* long before Brecht:

> Fright is a suddenly aroused fear that confuses the mind. Similar to fright is the feeling of being *struck* by something, which *stops us short* (but still does not throw us into confusion) and rouses the mind to collect its thoughts for reflection; it is the stimulus to *astonishment* (which already involves reflection). This does not happen so easily to experienced people; but it is the role of art to represent ordinary things from an aspect that makes them striking.

You see? Nothing new under the sun. By the way, I can recommend Kant's *Anthropology*, especially the third book, 'On the Appetitive Power' (where the above excerpt comes from) to all actors and directors. It's a treasure trove, full to the brim with ideas about acting and self-reflection, and compellingly written. The *Verfremdungseffekt* arouses a certain kind of attention in the spectator in an emotional and intelligent way. When the spectator is watching an activity that is more or less normal, he has an 'aha!-experience' if he knows more than the figure he is watching, even if it's only something like: 'But what he's doing's wrong!' Or: 'Serves him right!' The spectator's opinion about the action is independent from the figure or actor's opinion, and empowers and frees the spectator to react in the way he wishes or the way he must. A successful *Verfremdungseffekt* makes the spectator a little smarter and gives him a feeling of superiority. And it's fun, too.

Concerning *Gestus*: what does it mean and why is it important? The *Gestus*, or the stance that someone takes towards a situation, does not always agree with the meaning [*Sinn*] of the opinions and thoughts expressed in the situation. You can put it this way: stance [*Verhalten*] is of primary importance and changes the verbal statement if necessary. Take the line 'That's wonderful'. It expresses that something is agreeable, good-looking, exciting – it praises something. But if I say the line this way [demonstrated during the seminar], the line suddenly takes on the opposite meaning through my disapproving stance. It says: damn it, *merde*, shit. Another example: a man begs his girlfriend to surrender herself to him and, in saying no, she allows him everything. This 'no' is really a 'yes', because her feelings change her stance, which in turn changes the meaning of this decisive answer. What's true at the theatre is true in life: the speaker's stance takes precedence over the meaning of the text, the first subordinates the second. Every text, every spoken thought can be manipulated. 'The truth is concrete' means that it asserts itself either perceptibly or covertly.

Of course, Brecht required that his actors master breathing, vocal and physical technique. Much was demanded of us and we had to deliver. And Brecht made sure that every line was spoken with great lightness. The effort that stood behind our performance was not allowed to be seen. I wasn't always successful at this.

Berlin, 3 February 1956

Dear Schall,

I hear that the tent scene in *Courage* is suffering because you exaggerate Eilif's drunkenness. It's not good for this scene if the young man appears to be bedraggled in some way. The drink should just loosen his tongue and nothing further.

When he's looking at the map he should appear especially interested. In a word: a brilliant career seems to lie before him.

Hopefully you'll let the naturalness that you strive for in other roles help you in playing Eilif. Please correct Eilif <u>without</u> me. I'll only be able to study the production again once it goes on tour.

cordially yours,

brecht

Some actors are hyperactive [*Zappelphilipps*] and others are bards. Many actors, including remarkable ones, are aloof from their true duties and the real pleasures of acting, remaining imperfect in their movement or speech. Brecht's intention was to add his suggestions to the intellectual enterprise of theatre and develop it as a humanising stimulus capable of reaching everyone on earth, even the stubborn unbelievers (except those people from every walk of life who are either already dead while they are living, lack a belief in progress or are just plain stupid). Sooner or later, the prospects for his dialectical/epic theatre would have been bleak under any government, because he strove towards a model of community that valued and enabled human communication. His hope was that through performance, personal progress could be felt a part of worldwide human progress, menacing dangers and a threatening future weakened, that common paths into the future be found, even if they must be traversed as individuals. He wanted us to internalise the action at the theatre and then externalise it once again as a serious game with ourselves, as an attempt to focus the system of lenses through which we see society on a different point. *Perdu.*

Great efforts, minor deeds
Which will weigh the graver?
Soldiers still saw the light in the tunnel
Before falling silent.

ADDENDA

Seminars

BERGEN, NORWAY
BERGEN INTERNATIONAL FESTIVAL
Guest performance of the Berliner Ensemble, 22–28 May 1974

LONDON, ENGLAND
EDINBURGH, OXFORD, MANCHESTER, LEICESTER
ROSE BRUFORD COLLEGE
Solo tour, 8–19 January 1981

SYDNEY, AUSTRALIA
NIMROD THEATRE
MELBOURNE, ADELAIDE FESTIVAL
Solo tour, 5–21 March 1982

NEW YORK, USA
ACTORS' STUDIO and YALE UNIVERSITY
HAROLD CLURMANN THEATER, LUCILLE LORTEL THEATER, THE
POETRY CENTER, 92nd STREET Y
THEATRE PROJECT, BALTIMORE, HARVARD UNIVERSITY, BOSTON
UNIVERSITY OF ILLINOIS AT URBANA-CHAMPAIGN
Solo tour, 12–18 February 1985

MILAN, ITALY
CIVICO SCUOLA D'ARTE DRAMATICO 'PICCOLO TEATRO',
PICCOLO TEATRO DI MILANO, TEATRO LIRICO, MILAN
Solo guest performance/Guest performance of the Berliner
Ensemble, 9–18 December 1985

TORONTO, CANADA

UNIVERSITY OF TORONTO, ROYAL ALEXANDRA THEATRE

MELBOURNE INTERNATIONAL CONFERENCE AND THEATRE FESTIVAL

Solo guest performance / Guest performance of the Berliner
Ensemble, 21–26 October 1986

TEL AVIV, ISRAEL

JERUSALEM FESTIVAL

TEL AVIV UNIVERSITY

Solo guest performance / Guest performance of the Berliner
Ensemble, 20 May–10 June 1989

DELPHI, GREECE

THIRD INTERNATIONAL MEETING ON ANCIENT GREEK DRAMA

Solo guest performance, 24–28 June 1989

Roles Performed

Theatre (a Selection)
1946–48 – Magdeburg Municipal Theatre
Sebastian in Shakespeare's *Twelfth Night*
Hans Hartwig in Max Halbe's *Jungend* [Youth]
The Queen's Page in Schiller's *Don Carlos*
Michael Mews in Fritz Stavenhagen's *Mutter Mews*
Tonio in Heinz Hull's *Mutter*

1948–1950 – Stadttheater, Frankfurt an der Oder
Don Carlos in Schiller's *Don Carlos*
Leon in Franz Grillparzer's *Thou Shalt Not Lie*
Pupil in Goethe's *Faust I*
Alcest in Goethe's *Die Mitschuldigen*
Gerald Croft in J. B. Priestley's *An Inspector Calls*
Salieri in Alexander Pushkin's *Mozart and Salieri*
Lomov in Anton Chekhov's *The Marriage Proposal*
Mortimer in Schiller's *Mary Stuart*

1951–52

Kandybar in Alexander Korneichuk's *Holunderwäldchen*
Wolfgang Hederle in Paul Herbert Freyer's *Auf verlorenem Posten*

from 1952 (at the Berliner Ensemble unless otherwise specified)

1952   Eilif in Brecht's *Mother Courage*
1952   Ruprecht in Kleist's *The Broken Jug*
1952   José in *Señora Carrar's Rifles*
1952   Hermann in Strittmatter's *Katzgraben*
1954   Japanese Commander in *Hirse für die Achte* by Lo Ding, Tschang Fan and Tschu Dschin-nan
1955   Johannes Hörder in Becher's *Winter Battle*
1956   Shawn Keogh in Synge's *The Playboy of the Western World*
1957   Andrea in Brecht's *Life of Galileo*
1957   Sun in Brecht's *The Good Person of Sezuan*
1958   Alexei in Vishnevski's *Optimistic Tragedy*
1959   Arturo Ui in Brecht's *The Resistible Rise of Arturo Ui*
1962   Rigault in Brecht's *Days of the Commune*
1963   Philosopher in *The Messingkauf Dialogues*
1964   Coriolanus in Brecht's *Coriolanus*
1965   Oppenheimer in Kipphardt's *In the Matter of J. Robert Oppenheimer*
1967   Fairchild in Brecht's *Man Equals Man*
1968   Slift in Brecht's *Saint Joan of the Stockyards*
1970   Woyzeck in Büchner's *Woyzeck*
1971   Shlink in Brecht's *In the Jungle of Cities*
1971   Cardinal Barbarini in Brecht's *Life of Galileo*
1972   Heracles in Hack's *Omphale*
1973   Sergei Ivagin in Heiner Müller's *Cement*
1976   Puntila in Brecht's *Mr Puntila and his Man Matti*
1976   Azdak in Brecht's *The Caucasian Chalk Circle*
1977   Karl Marx in Günter Kaltofen and Hans Pfeifer's *Salut an alle – Marx* (Theater im Palast, Berlin)
1978   Ziffel in Brecht's *Conversations in Exile* (Theater im Palast, Berlin)

1978   Galileo in Brecht's *Life of Galileo*

1979   Gau Dsu in Braun's *Großer Frieden* [Great Peace]

1982   Faustus in Eisler's *Johann Faustus*

1983   Volpone in Jonson's *Volpone* (Theater im Palast, Berlin)

1984   King John in Shakespeare's *King John* (Theater im Palast, Berlin)

1985   Tersites in Shakespeare's *Troilus and Cressida*

1985   Edgar in Strindberg's *Dance of Death* (Theater im Palast, Berlin)

1987   Fatzer in Brecht's *Demise of the Egoist Johann Fatzer*

1987   Baal in Brecht's *Baal*

1990   Elector in Kleist's *The Prince of Homburg*

1990   The Devil in Hofmannsthal's *Jedermann* [*Everyman*] (Salzburger Festspiele)

1990   Man in lift in Heiner Müller's *Der Auftrag* [The Mission] (Schloßparktheater, Berlin)

1991   Wang in Brecht's *The Good Person of Sezuan*

1991   Krapp in Beckett's *Krapp's Last Tape* (Theater im Palast, Berlin)

1992   Man in Eduardo Galeano's *Memory of Fire* (Volksbühne, Berlin)

1992   Ill in Dürrenmatt's *Besuch der alten Dame* (Schloßparktheater, Berlin)

1994   Various roles in Goran Stefanovski's *Brecht in Exile* (Moving Theatre, London)

1994   Creon in Brecht's adaptation of *Antigone* (Co-Production Ruhrfestspiele, Recklinghausen, Zürich, Lausanne)

1996   Thoas in Goethe's *Iphigenie* (Théâtre Vidy, Lausanne/ Ruhrfestspiele)

1996   Stalin/Corionlanus in Heiner Müller's *Germania 3*

1999   Theodor Bruch in Christoph Hein's *Bruch* (Theater 89, Berlin)

Solo Programmes

1977   *Vom Lachen über die Welt zum Leben mit der Welt* [*From* laughing at the world to living with the world]

1980 *Von den Sterbenden. Von den Gestorbenen. Von den Lebenden* [*On the Dying. On the Dead. On the Living*]

1984 *Fragen. Klagen. Antworten* [*Questions. Complaints. Answers*]

1986 *Lebensabende* (Beckett and Brecht)

1989 *Laute Leute oder Jetzt reicht's aber!* [*Noisy Neighbours or That's Quite Enough!*]

1997 *EINSgegenEINS oder ICHHAbRECHT*

1999 Evening Goethe Recital

Radio

I. Rundfunk Berlin [Radio Berlin]

1953 *Señora Carrar's Rifles*

1953 *Unser Staat (Katzgraben)*

1954 *BB-Sendung* [Bertolt Brecht Programme]

1960 *Das neue Gedicht* [The new poem]

1960 *Hirse für die Achte*

1960 *Atelier und Bühne* [Studio and Stage]

1960 *Tyrannen und Tyrallalas*

1962 *Das andere Ufer* [The other bank]

1963 *Zu Gast bei Ekkehard Schall* [At home with Ekkehard Schall]

1963 *Mit Ilo durch alle Kurven*

1964 *Baal / Jacob Apfelböck*

1966 *Zu 'Coriolan'* [On *Coriolanus*]

1965 *65. Geburtstag Ernst Busch* [Ernst Busch's 65th Birthday]

1966 *Konzert (Sprecher)* [Speaker in Concert]

1966 *The Trial of Lucullus*

1967 *Konzert (Sprecher)* [Speaker in Concert]

1967 *Schatzkästlein* – Becher

1967 *Medea*

1968 *Kalifornische Ballade* [California Ballads]

1968 *Schatzkästlein* – Heine

1969 *The Ocean Flight*

II. Rundfunk Leipzig [Radio Leipzig]

1963   *Requiem for Lumumba* – Dessau
1965   German Symphony – Eisler
1965   *Jüdische Chronik* [Jewish Chronicle]
1966   Concert: Dessau – Schwaen
1966   Concert: Stravinsky
1966   Concert: Dessau
1967   *Jüdische Chronik* [Jewish Chronic]
1968   *Invocacion*
1968   Concert: Dorn
1969   Concert: Schoenberg
1969   Concert: Schwaen
1969   Concert: Dessau
1972   Concert: Schoenberg

LPs
1961   *Winter Battle*
1963   *Brecht Evening*
1963   *The Condemnation of Lucullus*
1964   *Das kleine Mahagonny* [The short *Mahagonny*]
1965   German Symphony – Eisler
1965   *Señora Carrar's Rifles*
1965   A Portrait of Ekkehard Schall
1966   *Hymnus 1959* – Dessau
1966   *Jüdische Chronik* [Jewish Chronicle]
1967   *Mother Courage*
1967   *Von der Natuer der Menschen* [On Human Nature]
1967   *The Caucasian Chalk Circle*
1969   *Songs and Chorales for plays* – Hosalla
1969   Fairy Tales – Wilhelm Hauff
1970   *The Days of the Commune*
1970   *Requiem for Lumumba* – Dessau

Television
1953   *Don Juan or the Stone Guest*
1960   *The Visions of Simone Machard*

1960   *Widowers' Houses* – Shaw
1961   *Daß ein gutes Deutschland blühe*
1961   *La Mandragola*
1961   *Guido Teller*
1961   *Napoleon in New Orleans*
1962   *Josef und alle seine Brüder*
1962   *Fetzers Fluch*
1962   *Parteiprogramm der SED*
1963   *Parteiprogramm der SED*
1963   *Junge Kunst*
1963   *Aus der Schule geplaudert*
1963   *Wolf unter Wölfen*
1964   *Rendezvous am Wochenende*
1964   *Künstlerporträt Manfred Wekwerth*
1964   *Woyzeck*
1965   *Guten Abend, Willi Schwabe*
1965   *Im Blickpunkt*
1965   *Paris 35*
1965   *Aus London zurück* (Berliner Ensemble) [Back from London]
1965   *Willst Du Dir ein hübsches Leben zimmern*
1965   *Becher-Sendung*
1966   *Ende der Anfrage*
1966   *The Condemnation of Lucullus*
1966   Scenes from *Matrosen von Cattaro*
1966   *Faust I* and *II*
1966   *Die deutschen Dinge*
1967   *Television*
1967   *Frühling 21*
1967   *Meine besten Freunde*
1967   *Geduld der Kühnen*
1967   *The Visions of Simone Machard*
1969   *Ljubow Jarowaja*
1972   *The Caucasian Chalk Circle*
1973   *Porträt Barbara Dittus*
1974   *The Resistible Rise of Arturo Ui*

1973   Interview partner
1973   *Pionerrevue*
1974   *Festveranstaltung (Neues Jugendgesetz)*
1977   *Goldene Zeiten*
1981   *Er liebt sie unendlich – Tchaikovsky*

Film

1956   *Wo Wir nicht sind . . . [Berlin-Ecke Schönhauser]*
1956   *Der Schein* Parts I and II
1958   *Hassan und der reiche Kaufmann Machmud*
1958   *Das Lied der Matrosen*
1959   *Maibowle*
1959   *Trübe Wasser*
1959   *Mother Courage*
1959   *Josef und die Ostpenner*
1959   *Haus im Feuer*
1960   *Der Traum des Hauptmann Loy*
1963   *Die Rote Kamille*
1968   *Erklärung eines Wunders*
1968   *Engel im Visier*
1969   *Datum*
1969   *Zwei Söhne*
1970   *Lenin*
1971   *Karl Liebknecht – Trotz alledem*

Index of Play Titles

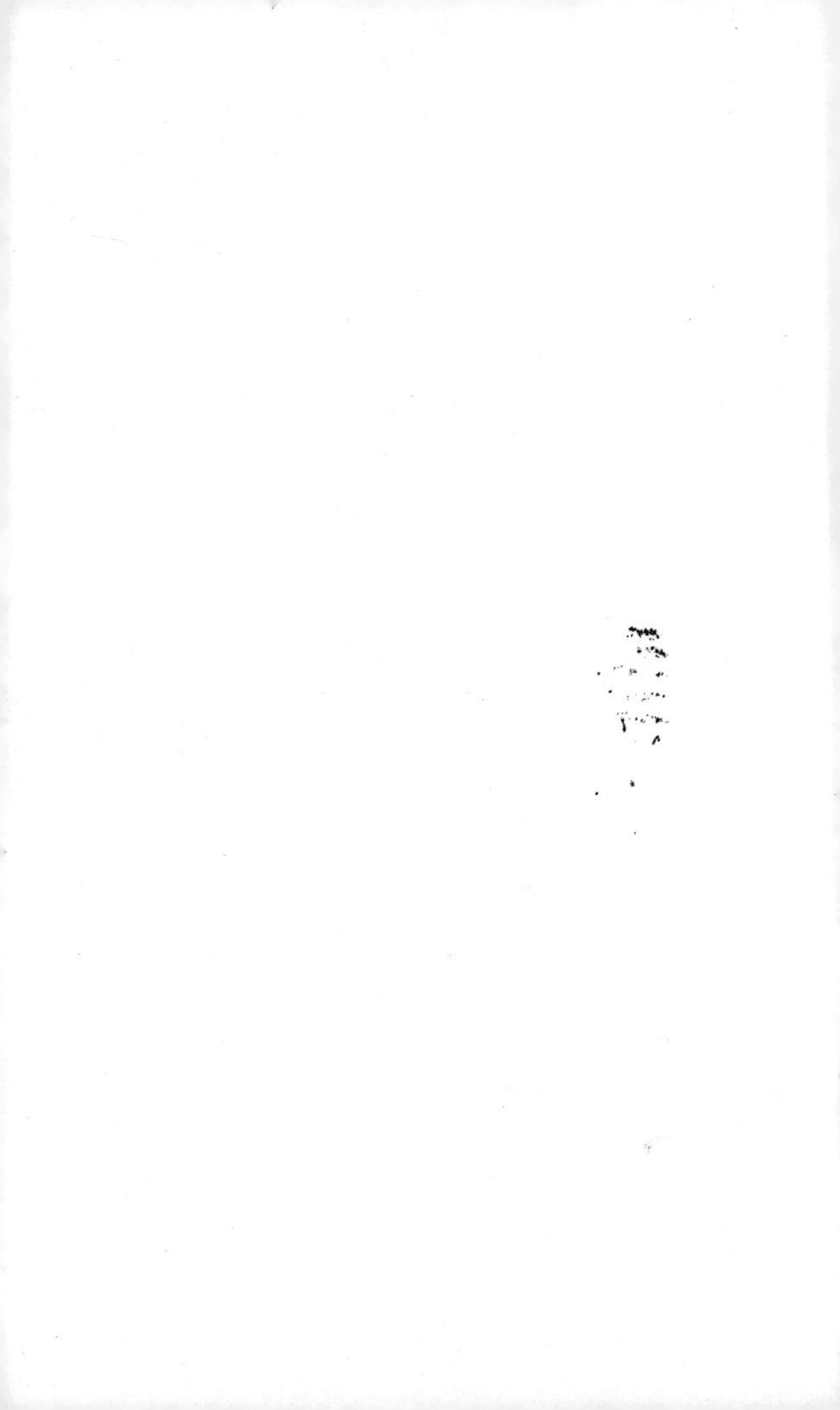